CRYPTOCURRENCY INVESTING 101

Understand Bitcoin, Avoid Mistakes, and Make Money Even If You Are An Absolute Beginner

Jordan Taylor

Also by Rivanna Heights Media

Pickleball Made Simple by Blake Foster

The Complete Beginner's Guide To ChatGPT by Ryan Harper

Contents

INTRODUCTION

In the past decade, the financial landscape has witnessed a seismic shift, spearheaded by the meteoric rise of cryptocurrencies. From Bitcoin's unprecedented surges to the nuanced dance of alt-currencies, meme coins, and non-fungible tokens (NFTs), this new era of digital assets redefines the essence of investment. As you stand on the brink of this revolutionary frontier, the opportunity to participate in the financial phenomena of our time beckons.

Embarking on this journey, you're in capable hands. With over eight years of asset management experience, advanced finance and investing degrees, and a career that straddles traditional finance and innovative data technologies, I bring a unique and comprehensive perspective to cryptocurrency investing. My expertise, further bolstered by certifications in several programming languages and hands-on experience developing secure data solutions, the foundation of blockchain, ensures you receive the most reliable and up-to-date information. You can trust my knowledge's depth and breadth to guide you on this exciting path.

Remember, this book is not just a theoretical exploration of cryptocurrency investing. It's a practical guide, meticulously crafted with a clear mission: to demystify the complex world of cryptocurrency investing for you. I aim to empower you with the knowledge, strategies, and tools necessary for informed decision-making, enabling you to confidently navigate this volatile market and potentially achieve substantial financial growth. You have the power to take control of your financial future.

As someone stepping into digital currencies, you seek a resource that transcends technical jargon and delivers practical investment wisdom. This book bridges that gap. It is written for you, ambitious individuals eyeing financial independence through informed and strategic investment in cryptocurrencies and other less traditional investments.

Adopting an approachable yet authoritative tone, this book leverages real-world examples and straightforward explanations to clarify intricate concepts. You can expect practical advice that you can apply directly to your investment endeavors, making your learning experience informative and immediately beneficial. This pragmatic approach gives you the confidence to make informed investment decisions.

This book is structured to guide you from the foundational principles of blockchain to advanced cryptocurrency investment strategies. It also covers crucial aspects like security best practices, legal considerations, and emerging trends that could shape the future of digital currencies.

With a unique blend of traditional financial acumen and in-depth blockchain knowledge, I offer practical and cutting-edge insights. This hands-on guide is drawn from real-world experiences and proven successes in the cryptocurrency markets.

By embarking on this reading, you are poised to learn and transform your understanding of cryptocurrency investing. You will emerge well-equipped to make savvy investment choices and be poised for financial growth in the ever-evolving digital economy. Let's begin this transformative journey together.

GETTING STARTED WITH CRYPTOCURRENCY

I n 2010, a programmer purchased two pizzas using 10,000 bitcoins, marking one of the first real-world transactions with cryptocurrency. This seemingly simple act was a precursor to the monumental shift that would soon sweep across the financial landscape, transforming how we perceive, interact with, and invest in the concept of money. Cryptocurrencies, born out of the need for decentralized and autonomous financial transactions, have challenged traditional banking systems and created a new asset class. In this chapter, we will explore the foundational elements of cryptocurrencies: what they are, how they operate, and their practical uses in today's economy.

1.1 What is Cryptocurrency? An In-Depth Introduction

Cryptocurrencies are digital or virtual currencies that use cryptography for security, making them nearly impossible to counterfeit or double-spend. They are distinguished by their decentralized nature, typically using blockchain technology to achieve consensus on transactions without a central authority. This revolutionary approach to currency is quite different from traditional fiat currencies, like the U.S. Dollar or Swiss Franc, which are issued and regulated by a central government.

The birth of cryptocurrency can be traced back to 2008 when an individual or group of individuals under the pseudonym Satoshi Nakamoto published the Bitcoin whitepaper. Bitcoin was introduced as a new form of currency and a radical new technology framework, promising a decentralized financial system where trust was established not by central authorities but through cryptographic proof and consensus.

Key Characteristics of Cryptocurrencies

Three intrinsic characteristics define cryptocurrencies: decentralization, immutability, and transparency. Decentralization means the network operates on a user-to-user (or peer-to-peer) basis. A decentralized network of computers (often called nodes) records transactions in a public ledger in multiple places at once. Immutability in the context of cryptocurrencies means once a transaction is recorded on the blockchain, it cannot be altered or deleted. This is crucial for preventing fraud and maintaining the integrity of the transaction history. Transparency means all transactions are visible to those who have access to the blockchain, ensuring that the currency's movement is always traceable and auditable by any party.

Types of Cryptocurrencies

While Bitcoin remains the most recognized cryptocurrency, thousands of alternatives exist, referred to as altcoins. Each cryptocurrency operates on its own underlying technology and has its unique value proposition. Some, like Ethereum, are not "currencies" but platforms that allow the creation of decentralized applications (dApps) using smart contracts. Others, like Ripple or Stellar, are designed to make cross-border transactions faster and cheaper. Then, there are tokens, which are typically created and distributed through Initial Coin Offerings (ICOs) and can represent a variety of assets or utilities within a specific ecosystem.

Use Cases of Cryptocurrencies

The use cases for cryptocurrencies have expanded exponentially since the advent of Bitcoin. Beyond just serving as a digital form of money, cryptocurrencies are now utilized for various practical applications. They facilitate cross-border payments, providing a faster, cheaper alternative to traditional methods such as wire transfers, which can be costly and slow, particularly in developing countries. Cryptocurrencies also play a significant role in remittances, where individuals working abroad send money back to their home countries.

Some argue that cryptocurrencies, particularly Bitcoin, can also act as a digital store of value and a hedge against inflation, which are properties of real assets and commodities. Perhaps most significantly, cryptocurrencies have emerged as a novel and compelling asset class for investment and speculation, offering opportunities for significant returns. While a risk, their volatility also provides unique opportunities for investors who understand market dynamics.

As we progress through this book, remember that cryptocurrency is vast and multifaceted. Whether used for daily transactions, powering decentralized applications, or as investment vehicles, cryptocurrencies are reshaping the financial landscape, offering a new paradigm of money and beyond. The journey into this dynamic field starts with understanding these fundamentals, setting the stage for deeper exploration into engaging with and benefitting from this exciting new world.

1.2 Understanding Blockchain: The Technology Behind Cryptos

Blockchain technology, often heralded as the backbone of cryptocurrencies, is a digital ledger whose ingenuity lies in ensuring security, transparency, and decentralization. Imagine a series of data blocks—each representing numerous transactions—linked and secured using cryptography. This chain of blocks is not stored in a central location but is instead distributed across a network of computers, making it exceptionally resistant to tampering and fraud. Each block contains a cryptographic hash of the previous block, a timestamp, and transaction data, typically represented as a Merkle tree. When a block's data is edited in any way, its hash changes significantly, thus alerting the system to potential fraud.

The process of conducting transactions on a blockchain starts with the transaction itself, which is proposed and then broadcast to a network of nodes. From there, the nodes undertake the task of validating the transaction. Miners come into play here, competing to solve a cryptographic puzzle that allows them to add a new block of transactions to the ledger. The first miner to solve the puzzle receives a reward in the form of cryptocurrency, incentivizing miners to maintain the network's integrity and speed. This process, known as proof of work, is typical of many cryptocurrencies, including Bitcoin. However, other consensus algorithms exist, such as proof of stake, which aims to achieve similar ends through different means, focusing on the number of coins miners hold as a determinant of their mining rights and rewards.

Beyond its role in powering cryptocurrencies, blockchain technology has profound implications across various sectors. Supply chain management offers unprecedented transparency and efficiency, allowing all parties to track goods from production to delivery without fear of data manipulation. This capability ensures that quality standards are met across the entirety of the chain, potentially reducing incidents of fraud and improving product recalls. In healthcare, blockchain can secure and manage sensitive patient data with fine-grained control over who can access what information and when. Moreover, in the realm of voting systems, blockchain could significantly enhance security and transparency, reducing the likelihood of vote tampering and boosting public trust in electoral processes.

However, blockchain is not without its challenges and limitations. Scalability remains a significant concern; as the number of transactions increases, the size of the blockchain grows, leading to slower transaction times and increased energy consumption. The Bitcoin network, for example, can handle only a fraction of the transactions per second that Visa can process, leading to potential delays and higher transaction fees during peak usage times. Furthermore, while secure, the proof of work consensus mechanism is incredibly energy-intensive. This has raised environmental concerns, particularly in regions where non-renewable energy sources power mining. Efforts to create more sustainable consensus algorithms are ongoing and vital to blockchain technologies' future scalability and acceptance.

As blockchain evolves, these challenges prompt ongoing debates and innovations, driving further research and development. Blockchain's dynamic nature ensures it remains at the forefront of technology, pushing the boundaries of what is possible within and beyond cryptocurrencies. This continuous evolution enhances blockchain's functionality and broadens its applicability, promising to instigate further transformations in how we interact with and trust digital systems in our increasingly interconnected world.

1.3 The Big Players: Bitcoin and Ethereum Explained

When discussing the landscape of cryptocurrencies, two names invariably dominate the conversation: Bitcoin and Ethereum. Each platform was designed with distinct purposes and technologies, and both have significantly influenced the cryptocurrency market.

Introduction to Bitcoin

Bitcoin, introduced to the world in a 2008 white paper by the pseudonymous creator Satoshi Nakamoto, is the first cryptocurrency ever created. This pioneering digital currency was developed in response to the 2008 financial crisis, proposing a new form of money independent of any central authority, thereby offering a decentralized alternative to traditional, government-issued currencies. The primary purpose of Bitcoin was to facilitate transactions directly between users without the need for intermediaries, using blockchain technology to ensure security and trust. Over the years, Bitcoin has gained immense popularity and has become seen as a medium of exchange and a store of value, often referred to as 'digital gold' due to its ability to hold value over time.

Understanding Ethereum

While Bitcoin was primarily created as an alternative to conventional currencies, Ethereum's conception aimed to revolutionize more than just how we view money. Launched in 2015 by Vitalik Buterin and his colleagues, Ethereum was designed to facilitate immutable, programmatic contracts and applications via its currency vehicle, Ether. This platform extends beyond the digital currency itself to include what are known as 'smart contracts,' self-executing contracts with the terms of the agreement directly written into code. Ethereum has also enabled the development and hosting of dApps on its blockchain. It supports many projects ranging from games to complex financial services, which can all operate without any central authority or single point of failure.

Differences between Bitcoin and Ethereum

The key difference between Bitcoin and Ethereum lies in their underlying purposes and the technologies they employ. Bitcoin's blockchain is primarily a ledger for recording transactions of its currency, optimized for security and reliability. Its scripting language is intentionally limited to essential functions. Ethereum, however, was created as a programmable blockchain that can process transactions and complex contracts and programs. This flexibility has made Ethereum the foundation for numerous applications across various industries, significantly broadening its use cases. While Bitcoin remains a single-layer currency used primarily for wealth storage and transfer, Ethereum's multi-functional platform supports a broader range of applications, including but not limited to its use as a digital currency.

Significance in the Market

Bitcoin and Ethereum have dramatically influenced the cryptocurrency ecosystem and the broader financial landscape. Bitcoin's emergence as the first blockchain-based cryptocurrency has paved the way for thousands of subsequent cryptocurrencies, with many fashioned on its blockchain technology or fundamental principles. Its market cap and price growth have helped cryptocurrency gain legitimacy in the eyes of the public and regulators, contributing to the development of related financial products like Bitcoin futures and Bitcoin exchange-traded-funds (ETFs).

On the other hand, Ethereum has played a crucial role in developing the ICO as a means of fundraising, a trend that peaked around 2017 and 2018. Its introduction of smart contracts has expanded the use cases of blockchain technology and spawned new finance industries, such as Decentralized Finance (DeFi), primarily built on Ethereum's network. The impact of Ethereum extends beyond finance, touching sectors like real estate and law, where smart contracts can provide more transparent, efficient, and direct dealings.

The influence of both Bitcoin and Ethereum continues to resonate through the market, driving ongoing innovation and adoption of blockchain technology. They have established substantial communities of developers and entrepreneurs dedicated to exploring new ways to leverage cryptocurrency platforms to solve existing challenges and innovate for future needs. As these technologies evolve, their foundational role in the digital asset economy ensures their continued relevance and leadership in the space, shaping the direction of blockchain development and the broader technology landscape for years to come.

1.4 Setting Up Your Crypto Wallet: A Step-by-Step Guide

Navigating the world of cryptocurrencies begins with a fundamental step: setting up a crypto wallet. This digital wallet is your ledger for tracking cryptocurrencies and is your primary tool for executing transactions. Understanding the different types of wallets and their respective security features is crucial in making an informed decision that aligns with your needs.

Types of wallets

Crypto wallets come in various forms, each offering distinct advantages and levels of security. **Hardware wallets** like those offered by Ledger or Trezor resemble USB devices and provide offline storage for your cryptocurrencies. Their physical form factor is designed to maximize security; they remain disconnected from the internet most of the time, which shields them from online hacking attempts and makes them less susceptible to malware or virus infections. They are known as cold wallets because of their disconnection from the internet. On the other hand, **software wallets** are applications that can be installed on your computer or smartphone. They offer convenience and quick access, ideal for those who trade frequently. However, they are considered less secure than hardware wallets since they are connected to the internet. Because of this connectivity, they are known as hot wallets. Lastly, **paper wallets** are another type of cold storage. They are simply pieces of paper with your public and private keys printed. They can't be hacked online because they are not connected to the internet. However, you need to be very careful with them because if you lose or damage the paper, you could lose access to your cryptocurrency.

Choosing the right wallet

Selecting the appropriate wallet depends mainly on your interaction with cryptocurrencies. If your strategy involves holding large amounts of cryptocurrencies long-term, a hardware wallet or an adequately secured paper wallet might be the best choice due to its robust security features. Software wallets provide convenience for those actively trading or needing frequent access to send and receive cryptocurrencies. It's essential to consider the reputation of the wallet provider, focusing on factors like user reviews, company history, and the level of customer support. Security features such as two-factor authentication, multi-signature support, and regular software updates should also influence your decision. We will explore these considerations further as we dig deeper into securing cryptocurrency investments.

Setting up a wallet

Some investors opt not to set up wallets to avoid the responsibility of managing private keys and to rely instead on the security measures provided by **cryptocurrency exchanges** (more on exchanges later). However, if you set up a wallet, the next step involves configuring it properly.

For hardware wallets, this process includes plugging the device into your computer, installing the corresponding application, and setting a strong password or PIN. Most hardware wallets will generate a recovery phrase—a series of words in a specific order—that you must write down and store securely. This recovery phrase is crucial as it lets you restore your wallet on a new device if the original is lost, damaged, or stolen.

The setup process for software wallets is similar to that of hardware wallets and typically involves downloading and installing the software. During setup, you'll create a password and, in most cases, a recovery phrase. It is vital to ensure that any software wallet you download is from a reliable source to avoid malicious software designed to steal your funds.

Sending and receiving cryptocurrency

Sending and receiving cryptocurrencies are fundamental functions of any crypto wallet. To receive cryptocurrency, you must provide the sender with your wallet's public address. Think of this as your bank account number, but the address does not reveal your identity for cryptocurrencies unless linked through external information. This provides a degree of pseudonymity not available in traditional banking. It's crucial to ensure that the address is accurate when sharing it; even a tiny mistake can result in funds being irreversibly lost. When sending cryptocurrencies, you will enter the recipient's public address. Here, too, accuracy is paramount. Always double-check the address before confirming the transaction. Most wallets provide a feature to scan a QR code, which minimizes the risk of error when entering a recipient's address.

Security should be your top priority during these transactions. Always ensure your internet connection is secure, and consider using a VPN to add a layer of security. Regularly update your wallet software to protect against vulnerabilities, and never share your private keys or recovery phrases with anyone. By diligently following these steps, you can securely manage your digital assets and confidently navigate the complex world of cryptocurrencies.

1.5 Navigating Crypto Exchanges: Where and How to Buy Crypto

Understanding the arena where cryptocurrencies are traded is pivotal for anyone looking to invest in this digital asset class. Cryptocurrency exchanges are platforms where you can buy, sell, or exchange cryptocurrencies for other digital currencies or traditional currencies like U.S. dollars (USD) or euros (EUR). These platforms are fundamental to executing any cryptocurrency investment strategy, and knowing how they operate can significantly enhance your trading efficiency and security.

Types of exchanges

The cryptocurrency exchange ecosystem is broadly divided into centralized exchanges (CEX) and decentralized exchanges (DEX). Centralized exchanges are managed by a company that provides a platform for trading cryptocurrencies. This type of exchange is user-friendly and provides more reliability in terms of speed and features like customer support and enhanced trading tools. However, they require users to entrust their funds to the company, posing potential security risks if the company's system is breached or faces operational issues that could lead to insolvency, potentially resulting in the loss of funds stored on the exchange.

On the other hand, decentralized exchanges operate without a central authority. Trades occur directly between users (peer-to-peer) through an automated process. This setup enhances security by eliminating the risk of hacking associated with centralized exchanges. However, DEXs can be less user-friendly and often lack the volume, speed, and liquidity their centralized counterparts provide. Choosing between a CEX and a DEX can significantly influence your trading experience. Centralized exchanges are generally recommended for beginners due to their ease of use, while more experienced traders might value the security and anonymity provided by decentralized exchanges.

Creating an account

Now that we understand the basics setting up an account on a cryptocurrency exchange is the first step toward trading and owning cryptocurrencies. The process typically involves registering with an exchange using your identification information and creating login credentials. Most centralized exchanges require you to complete a Know Your Customer (KYC) process. This process involves providing personal information and identification documents. This is a regulatory requirement intended to prevent illegal activities like money laundering. While it might seem cumbersome, completing KYC is crucial for the security of your transactions and compliance with financial regulations.

When creating your account, it's essential to adopt best security practices. This includes using a robust and unique password for your exchange account, enabling two-factor authentication (2FA), and securing your linked email account. These steps protect your account from unauthorized access and potential security breaches.

How to buy cryptocurrency

Purchasing cryptocurrency involves a few critical steps. First, you need to deposit funds into your exchange account. This can typically be done through bank transfers, credit or debit card transfers, or even via PayPal on some exchanges. Once your account is funded, you can start buying cryptocurrencies. This process involves selecting a trading pair. For example, the trading pair would be BTC/USD if you wish to buy Bitcoin using USD.

On most cryptocurrency exchanges, you can place different types of orders. The most straightforward is a **market order**, where you buy or sell a cryptocurrency at the best available price in the current market. This type of order is executed immediately, but the exact cost may vary slightly from the one displayed due to market fluctuations.

Alternatively, you can use **limit orders** to specify the exact price you want to buy or sell a cryptocurrency. For example, if you believe that the price of Bitcoin will drop to a certain level before rising again, you can place a limit buy order at that lower price. Similarly, if you own a cryptocurrency and want to sell it once it reaches a specific price point, you can set a limit on the sell order. Limit orders give you more control over the price you pay or receive for a cryptocurrency but may not be executed if the market price doesn't reach your specified level.

Understanding these order types and how they work is crucial in managing your investments effectively and minimizing risks. By using market and limit orders strategically, you can take advantage of price movements in the market and make informed decisions about when to buy or sell cryptocurrencies. Some investors prefer always to use market orders, assuming that the difference in price over a short period is not worth the extra analysis and effort. Conversely, others opt for limit orders to mitigate the impact of the bid-ask spread—the difference between the highest price a buyer is willing to pay and the lowest price a seller is willing to accept. These investors aim to achieve a more favorable entry or exit price using limit orders.

Another vital aspect to consider is the fees associated with trading. Most exchanges charge a percentage of each transaction as fees, which can vary based on factors like the type of order, the volume of trade, and market conditions. It's essential to carefully consider these fees, as they can impact your overall profitability. Additionally, some exchanges offer lower fees for higher volume trades or for holding their native cryptocurrency tokens, which can be used to pay fees at a discount. Furthermore, subscribing to a higher service level, such as "Pro," on certain exchanges can unlock lower fees and additional features. Understanding these fee structures can help optimize your trading strategy and maximize your returns.

Withdrawing and depositing

The ability to move your cryptocurrencies in and out of exchanges is crucial for managing your investments. Depositing involves transferring cryptocurrencies from your wallet to your exchange account. This process typically involves generating a deposit address from the exchange and sending your cryptocurrencies to this address. It's crucial to double-check the address to ensure that the coins are being sent to the correct place, as mistakes could result in irreversible losses.

Withdrawing cryptocurrencies follows a similar process but in reverse. You need to generate a receiving address from your wallet and enter this address into the exchange to transfer funds from your exchange account to your wallet. This step is critical, especially if you are using a hardware wallet or any form of cold storage. Security is paramount during these transactions. Always ensure that you are operating on a secure and private internet connection. Additionally, use allowlisting features on exchanges that allow only pre-approved addresses to withdraw funds, adding an extra layer of security.

Navigating cryptocurrency exchanges efficiently requires understanding the types of exchanges, the process of creating and securing an account, the trading mechanisms, and the intricacies of handling transactions securely. By mastering these elements, you can take confident steps towards building and managing your cryptocurrency portfolio effectively.

1.6 Your First Investment: Steps to Buying Your First Bitcoin

When venturing into cryptocurrency, particularly Bitcoin, the initial investment marks a pivotal moment in your financial journey. Understanding the market dynamics and making informed decisions can significantly impact your success in this volatile and innovative market. Before initiating your first transaction, engaging in thorough market research is imperative. This involves analyzing current trends, historical data, and future projections to understand how Bitcoin behaves. This research will inform your decisions and help you anticipate potential market movements.

Market research should include monitoring Bitcoin's performance indices and understanding the factors that influence price fluctuations, such as regulatory news, technological advancements, and changes in the economic landscape. Platforms like CoinMarketCap and CryptoCompare can provide comprehensive insights and real-time data to aid your analysis. Additionally, following reputable financial news sources and participating in community discussions can offer deeper insights and diverse perspectives that enhance your understanding of the market.

Once you grasp the market conditions, the next step is to determine the amount of money you are willing to invest. This decision should align with your financial goals, risk tolerance, and the market research you've conducted. It is generally advisable to start with an amount you are comfortable potentially losing, given the inherent risks associated with volatile markets like those associated with cryptocurrencies.

The concept of **dollar-cost averaging** can be beneficial here. This investment strategy involves dividing the total amount to be invested across periodic purchases of a target asset to reduce the impact of volatility on the overall purchase. For example, let's say you've decided to invest \$1,000 in Bitcoin. Instead of investing the entire amount simultaneously, you could implement dollar-cost averaging by dividing the investment over several weeks or months. This approach allows you to purchase Bitcoin at different price points over time, smoothing out the impact of price fluctuations. For instance, you might invest \$200 every month for five months, regardless of whether the price of Bitcoin is high or low at the time of each purchase. The advantage here is twofold: it mitigates some of the emotional perils of investing, and it can potentially lower the cost basis of your investment over time if the market's direction is not in your favor.

Completing your first Bitcoin transaction involves several critical steps. First, you need to choose a reputable cryptocurrency exchange that aligns with your needs in terms of ease of use, security features, and transaction fees. Once registered and any necessary KYC processes are passed, deposit your initial investment amount into your exchange account. Following this, navigate to the exchange's trading interface, select the appropriate trading pair and order type, and follow the exchange's prompts to complete the order. You will now own your first cryptocurrency and be able to monitor its value.

After purchasing Bitcoin, it is crucial to consider the security and management of your investment. While keeping your Bitcoin in exchange for trading purposes is convenient, transferring your funds to a personal cryptocurrency wallet is safer, especially if you plan to hold on to your Bitcoin as a long-term investment. Transfacing your Bitcoin involves generating a receiving address from your wallet and withdrawing your Bitcoin from the exchange to this address. This step is critical and requires meticulous attention to ensure the address is correctly entered to avoid losing funds.

Monitoring your investment is an ongoing process. This includes keeping track of the performance of your Bitcoin, staying updated with cryptocurrency news that could affect market prices, and adjusting your investment strategy based on market conditions and personal financial goals. Tools like price alert apps and portfolio trackers can be invaluable in helping you stay informed and make timely decisions.

Investing in Bitcoin presents an exciting opportunity to participate in the growth of a transformative financial technology. However, it requires careful planning, ongoing education, and a clear understanding of your financial goals and risk tolerance. By following these steps, you can make your first Bitcoin investment with greater confidence and clarity, setting the stage for future financial exploration in the ever-evolving world of cryptocurrencies. As you expand your portfolio and gain more experience, these initial steps will serve as a foundation for a robust investment strategy tailored to navigate the complexities and capitalize on the opportunities within the cryptocurrency market.

Remember that these steps can also be used to buy altcoins, which are similar to buying Bitcoin. Depending on your exchange, you will follow the same steps: selecting a reputable exchange, completing any necessary KYC procedures, depositing funds, and navigating the trading interface to choose the appropriate trading pair and order type. Whether you are purchasing Ethereum, Litecoin, or any other altcoin, these steps will guide you through the transaction. However, the availability of specific altcoins can vary between exchanges, so it's essential to ensure the exchange you select supports the altcoin(s) you wish to buy.

1.7 Knowledge Check: Test Your Understanding

What distinguishes cryptocurrencies from traditional fiat currencies like the U.S. Dollar?

a) Cryptocurrencies are issued and regulated by a central government

b) Cryptocurrencies use decentralized networks and cryptography for security

c) Cryptocurrencies are physical coins and banknotes

d) Cryptocurrencies can be double-spent easily

Who published the Bitcoin whitepaper in 2008 outlining the concept of a decentralized digital currency?

a) Vitalik Buterin

b) Charlie Lee

c) Satoshi Nakamoto

d) Roger Ver

Answers:

1 – b) Cryptocurrencies use decentralized networks and cryptography for security

2 – c) Satoshi Nakamoto

INVESTMENT STRATEGIES AND RISK MANAGEMENT

Now that you know how to execute cryptocurrency purchases, let's transition to understanding investment strategies and risk management. Grasping the strategic landscape becomes crucial as you delve deeper into cryptocurrency investing. While the crypto market's volatility presents significant opportunities for substantial gains, it also poses unique challenges that require informed decision-making, meticulous planning, and the ability to remain mentally grounded amidst fluctuations to avoid overreaction. This chapter aims to equip you with the knowledge to discern between different investment strategies—particularly long-term versus short-term—and to select the one that aligns best with your financial goals, risk tolerance, and lifestyle.

2.1 Long-Term vs. Short-Term: Strategic Planning for Crypto Investments

Investment strategies in the cryptocurrency domain can broadly be categorized into two distinct approaches: long-term and short-term investments. These strategies differ not only in their temporal outlook but also in their operational tactics, risk exposure, and potential returns.

Understanding Investment Horizons

Long-term investment strategies are often synonymous with a **buy-and-hold** philosophy. This approach involves purchasing cryptocurrencies and holding onto them for several years or even decades. Investors who adopt this strategy typically believe in the long-term potential of their investments to yield substantial returns. They are less concerned with short-term fluctuations and more focused on the cumulative gains over the years. The rationale behind this strategy is that, despite the volatility of the crypto market, the overall trajectory of technology-driven assets like Bitcoin has historically been positive.

Conversely, short-term investment strategies are characterized by the frequent buying and selling of cryptocurrencies over shorter intervals—ranging from a few minutes to several months. This method is often driven by the goal to capitalize on the market's volatility by buying low and selling high in quick successions. Short-term investors, or traders, utilize various tools to forecast potential price movements and make swift decisions that align with slight market shifts.

Pros and Cons of Each Strategy

Each investment strategy has its advantages and disadvantages. Long-term investments typically require less time and energy daily, as these investors are not actively trading based on market fluctuations. In many jurisdictions, they can also benefit from lower tax rates on long-term capital gains. However, the downside includes the opportunity cost of locking in capital for an extended period and enduring the psychological stress of witnessing significant dips without immediate action.

While short-term investments offer the possibility of quick returns, they require constant market analysis and an active management style. This can be both time-consuming and stressful. Furthermore, the fees associated with frequent trading can accumulate, reducing the net gain from the investment activities. Moreover, short-term gains are taxed at higher rates than long-term gains, which can further erode profits.

Choosing the Right Strategy

Selecting the appropriate investment strategy is a highly personalized decision influenced by individual financial goals, risk tolerance, and market understanding. For those who prefer a more hands-off approach and strongly believe in the future of cryptocurrencies, a long-term strategy might be more suitable. This approach is less about timing the market and more about time in the market, letting the inherent value of suitable investments appreciate over time.

A short-term strategy could be more rewarding for others who perhaps understand market trends and derive satisfaction from active trading. This choice should also consider personal circumstances such as financial needs, lifestyle preferences, and the ability to withstand market volatility.

Case Studies

Consider the following real-life examples to illustrate these strategies in action. An investor who purchased Bitcoin in 2011 and held onto it until 2021 would have experienced a meteoric rise in value despite several market corrections. This investor benefited from a long-term strategy by not capitulating during high-volatility periods.

On the other hand, a trader who engaged in day trading Ethereum during the 2020 market upsurge might have capitalized on multiple price fluctuations within days or even hours, securing profits by timing the market effectively. However, this required constant market surveillance and a robust understanding of price indicators to make profitable trades quickly.

Both strategies have demonstrated potential for substantial returns but cater to different investor profiles and preferences. As you consider your entry into cryptocurrency investing, reflect on these narratives and assess which strategy aligns most closely with your financial goals and lifestyle. Remember, the choice of investment strategy affects potential returns and dictates the daily or long-term involvement required in managing your portfolio and, possibly, how much sleep you lose at night. Choose wisely, and let your strategy reflect your market outlook, financial goals, and personal circumstances.

2.2 Diversification Strategies in Cryptocurrency Investing

Beyond time-horizon strategies, diversification is a fundamental investment strategy crucial for managing risk in cryptocurrency investing. It aims to spread risk across various assets and minimize the impact of any single asset's poor performance on the overall portfolio. Diversification is crucial in mitigating risks associated with turbulent price movements in the volatile world of cryptocurrencies. By allocating investments across various cryptocurrencies and other asset types, investors can shield themselves from the adverse effects of any single investment's downturn.

Cryptocurrencies, characterized by their inherent volatility, can experience dramatic price swings influenced by regulatory news, technological advancements, market sentiment, and macroeconomic trends. While this volatility presents opportunities for high returns, it also poses substantial risks. Diversification helps manage these risks by spreading exposure across different assets. For instance, while one cryptocurrency may face regulatory challenges in a particular jurisdiction, another might benefit from technological advancements or positive market sentiment. This approach ensures that the negative impact of poor performance in one area may be balanced by positive performance elsewhere, leading to a more stable overall portfolio return.

However, it's essential to recognize that many assets in the digital asset class tend to move in the same direction, albeit to different magnitudes. Therefore, while diversification is a valuable risk management strategy, it may not fully mitigate the risks associated with broader market movements. Despite this, diversification remains an essential tool for investors seeking to improve the stability of their investment portfolios.

Methods to Diversify

When considering diversifying your cryptocurrency portfolio, think beyond just investing in different digital currencies. While it's beneficial to invest across various cryptocurrencies, including both established coins like Bitcoin and Ethereum and smaller altcoins, diversification can be enhanced by exploring investments across different sectors within the crypto market. Privacy coins, utility tokens, and security tokens, for instance, each serve distinct purposes and are influenced by other market factors. Privacy coins offer anonymity, which may be sought after in specific market environments; utility tokens can provide functional use cases in various projects; and security tokens are linked to real-world assets, potentially offering a bridge to more traditional investment environments.

Moreover, integrating non-crypto assets into your investment strategy can further diversify your portfolio. This might include traditional assets such as stocks, bonds, and real estate or alternative investments like commodities or art. The key is identifying assets not closely correlated with the cryptocurrency market. These assets can act as a hedge against crypto market volatility, providing stability and reducing the overall risk profile of your investment portfolio.

Rebalancing Your Portfolio

As markets change, so too will the composition of your portfolio. **Rebalancing** is generally considered an essential portfolio management process. Rebalancing involves adjusting your holdings to maintain desired asset allocation and risk levels. This practice is even more crucial in cryptocurrency investing due to the rapid price changes common within this market. For instance, if a particular cryptocurrency performs exceptionally well, it might start to constitute a more significant percentage of your portfolio than you initially intended, thereby increasing your exposure to risk if the market for that cryptocurrency suddenly declines.

Periodic rebalancing allows you to profit from high-performing investments and reinvest in underperforming areas, maintaining a balanced risk across your portfolio. This strategy can help you stay aligned with your investment goals, but it's essential to be mindful of the tax consequences, as selling assets can trigger capital gains taxes. Rebalancing should not be a daily or weekly task but a strategic decision made at set intervals or under specific conditions predefined in your investment strategy. Regularly scheduled reviews, whether quarterly, bi-annually, or annually, can help make informed decisions about when to buy more of an asset or sell off parts of your holdings.

There is some debate among investors about the necessity of rebalancing. Some argue it may not be necessary, as it involves selling high-performing assets and buying underperforming assets, which can seem counterintuitive. However, rebalancing should be considered as it can help manage risk and ensure that your portfolio remains diversified and aligned with your risk tolerance and investment objectives.

Ultimately, your financial goals, market conditions, and overall strategy should guide your decision to rebalance and the frequency of doing so. By carefully considering these factors, you can make informed decisions that support your investment portfolio's long-term health and stability.

Tools for Portfolio Management

Effective management of a diversified portfolio requires the right tools. Several software solutions and platforms can assist in tracking and managing your investments. Portfolio management tools specifically designed for cryptocurrency can help monitor your asset distribution, performance, and overall market trends. These tools often provide dashboards that display real-time balances, asset values, and the performance of individual investments, making it easier to see when your portfolio drifts from your target allocation.

Additionally, many of these tools offer features such as automatic rebalancing, which can help maintain your desired asset mix without needing to trade manually. Alerts can also be set up to notify you of significant market movements, providing opportunities to review and adjust your portfolio as necessary. With the right tools, maintaining a diversified investment portfolio is less daunting, allowing you to make more strategic decisions and respond effectively to market changes.

Incorporating these diversification strategies into your investment approach helps mitigate risk and positions you to capture growth across a broader range of assets. By understanding and implementing these strategies, you can navigate the complexities of the cryptocurrency markets more confidently, making informed decisions that align with your long-term financial goals.

Beyond the tools provided by exchanges, several external software solutions and platforms can further assist you. Websites like CoinMarketCap, CoinGecko, and TradingView offer extensive charting tools that provide detailed information about market trends and individual asset performance. These platforms often include features for **technical analysis** (more on that to come), such as indicators and historical data, which can help you make more informed decisions.

2.3 Understanding and Using Technical Analysis in Crypto Markets

Technical analysis is an important tool for anyone navigating the often volatile and unpredictable cryptocurrency markets. This method involves studying historical price and volume data to forecast future market behavior. Unlike **fundamental analysis**, which focuses on evaluating a security's intrinsic value based on economic and financial factors, technical analysis looks at patterns and trends in price movements and trading volumes to predict how prices will move. This approach can be compelling in the cryptocurrency market, where prices can be significantly influenced by trader psychology and sentiment.

Basics of Technical Analysis

At the core of technical analysis are three fundamental concepts: chart patterns, trend lines, and volume. Chart patterns help identify trends and predict future movements by depicting the historical performance of securities in graphical formats. Common chart types used in crypto trading include line charts, bar charts, and the more comprehensive candlestick charts. Each type provides different insights, with candlestick charts being valuable for showing price movements within a specific period, offering insights into market sentiment and potential price changes.

Trend lines are another pillar of technical analysis *(Image 2.1)*. They are solid lines drawn on charts representing the asset's trend and can indicate support and resistance levels. A support level is where the price tends to find support as it falls, which means it is more likely to bounce off this level than break through it. Conversely, a resistance level is where the price usually stops rising and may start to drop again. Identifying these levels can help traders decide about buying and selling, as they indicate potential points where prices could change direction.

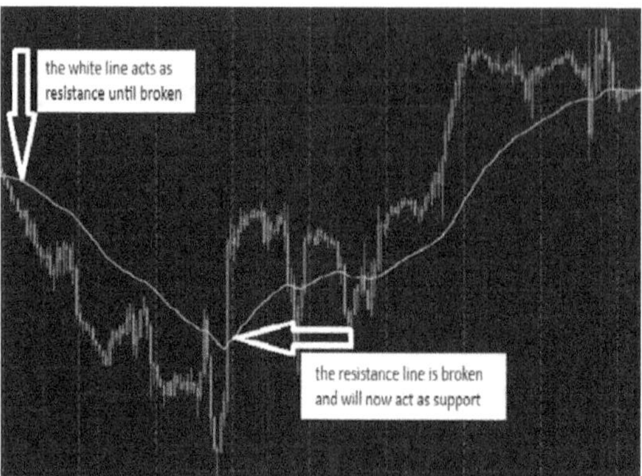

Image 2.1: Trend lines displayed on a chart

Volume, the total amount of a cryptocurrency traded in a given timeframe, is also crucial in confirming trends shown by chart patterns and trend lines. For example, a price movement accompanied by high volume is more likely to be sustainable. This is because high volume indicates strong interest in that price level, whether it's an upward or downward trend, suggesting that the price movement is backed by substantial trading activity.

Key Technical Indicators

Several technical indicators are widely utilized in cryptocurrency trading to aid investors in making informed decisions. **Moving averages** are among the most commonly employed indicators, smoothing out price data into a continuous line that facilitates trend identification *(Image 2.2)*. For instance, if Bitcoin's price remains above its 200-day moving average, it typically indicates a sustained upward trend. Additionally, comparing moving averages of different periods can provide further insights. For example, when the 50-day moving average crosses above the 200-day moving average, it suggests a potential uptrend in the asset's price.

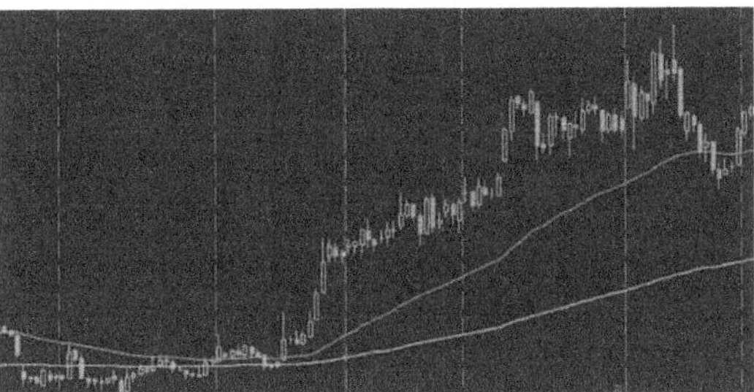

Image 2.2: 50-day and 200-day moving averages displayed on a trading platform

The **Relative Strength Index** (RSI) is another powerful tool that measures the speed and change of price movements on a scale of zero to 100 *(Image 2.3)*. Typically, an RSI above 70 may indicate that a cryptocurrency is overbought, while an RSI below 30 might suggest that it is oversold. This information can help traders predict when the market may turn.

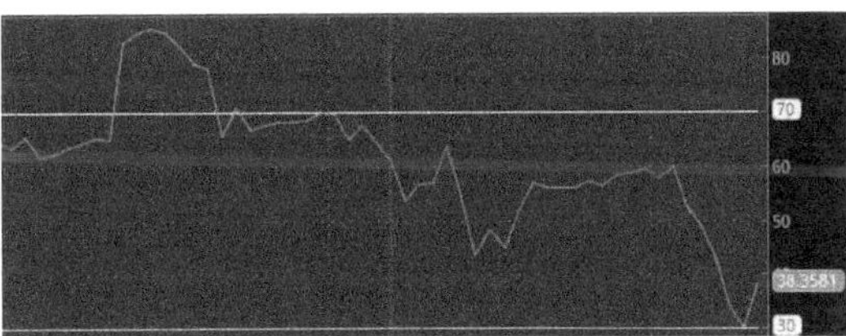

Image 2.3: Relative strength index displayed on a trading platform

The **Moving Average Convergence Divergence** (MACD) is a more sophisticated tool that helps traders understand whether the bullish or bearish movement is strengthening or weakening *(Image 2.4)*. It shows the relationship between two moving averages of a cryptocurrency's price. When the MACD crosses above its signal line, it could be bullish, while crossing below may suggest a bearish signal.

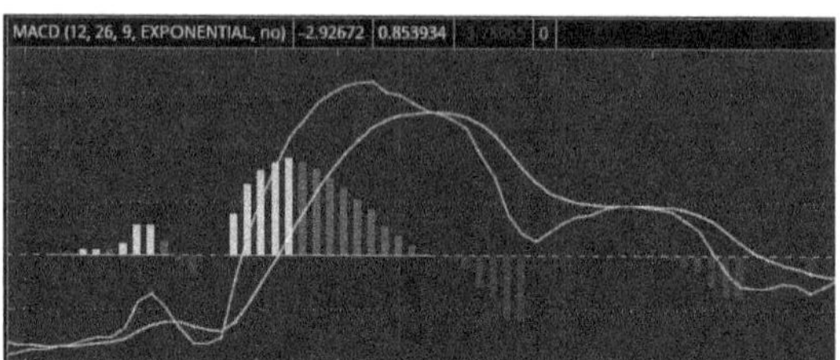

Image 2.4: Moving average convergence divergence displayed on a trading platform

Access to technical data for trading is readily available through cryptocurrency exchanges, financial news websites, and specialized trading platforms. These sources offer customizable charting tools, historical data, and a variety of technical indicators to analyze market trends, monitor price movements, and assess trading volumes. Additionally, desktop and mobile trading applications provide real-time market updates and advanced analysis features. For more in-depth insights, subscription-based services and financial analysis firms offer premium technical analysis tools for different trading strategies.

Chart Patterns and What They Signify

Recognizing and interpreting chart patterns is a skill that can significantly enhance your trading decisions. Patterns like "head and shoulders," "double top and bottom" *(Image 2.5)*, and 'triangles' can signal whether a trend will continue or reverse. For example, the head and shoulders pattern is often viewed as a reversal pattern that signals a potential shift from a bullish to a bearish trend. Similarly, double bottoms may indicate a turning point where the market could start to recover from a downtrend.

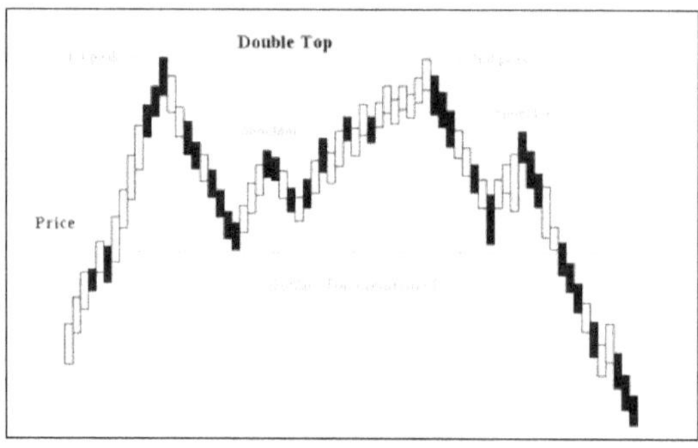

Image 2.5: Double top chart pattern example

Triangles are another pattern you might encounter, which can be symmetrical, ascending, or descending *(Image 2.6)*. These patterns are significant as they show a period where the price ranges narrow into a tighter area before eventually breaking out. The direction of the breakout can give clues about whether the price is likely to rise or fall, providing a strategic entry or exit point.

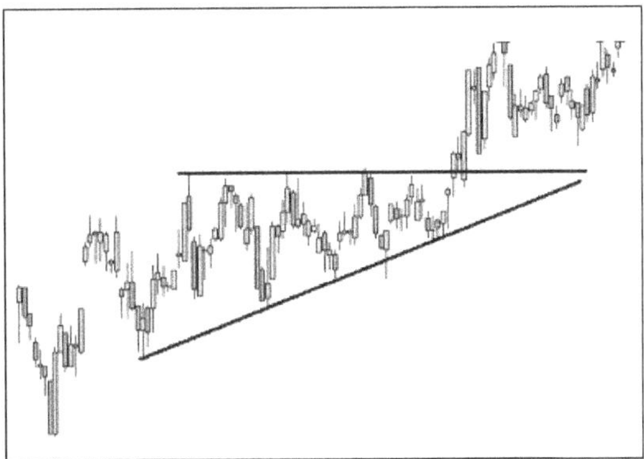

Image 2.6: Ascending triangle chart pattern example

Applying Technical Analysis

To apply technical analysis effectively, select a few key indicators and chart patterns you understand well and find intuitive. Monitor these indicators consistently and watch how they correlate with price movements. For practical application, let's consider a hypothetical scenario where you are tracking Ethereum. You notice that Ethereum has formed a double bottom pattern on the daily chart, and the RSI is below 30, suggesting that it is potentially oversold. Meanwhile, the MACD is beginning to show a bullish crossover. Based on this combination of technical signals, you might decide it's a good time to buy Ethereum, anticipating that the price will start an upward trend soon.

As you become more comfortable with these tools, you can start to combine them to refine your trading strategies. Remember, no indicator is foolproof. They are best used to support your decision-making process, combined with a solid understanding of market conditions and sound risk management practices. By mastering technical analysis, you equip yourself with the ability to make more informed and confident investment decisions in the dynamic world of cryptocurrency trading.

These are only some of the indicators available to traders. Understanding and mastering these basics is a great starting point, but there are many more tools and strategies within technical analysis. Exploring further resources and more advanced techniques is beneficial for those looking to deepen their knowledge. A good starting point for this deeper dive is Investopedia's guide to technical analysis, which offers comprehensive information on various indicators and how to use them effectively. By expanding your understanding, you can make more nuanced and informed trading decisions, enhancing your ability to navigate the complexities of the cryptocurrency markets.

2.4 Setting Stop-Loss Orders: A Safety Net for Your Investments

In the dynamic world of cryptocurrency trading, where market conditions can shift with startling speed, the utility of **stop-loss** orders emerges as a valuable tool in an investor's arsenal. A stop-loss order is an automatic instruction set to sell a cryptocurrency when it reaches a specific price, designed to limit an investor's loss on a position. This safety net mechanism prevents substantial financial losses during sudden market downturns. It is precious in the crypto market, known for its high volatility, where double-digit swings can occur within hours or even minutes.

How to Set Stop-Loss Orders

Setting up a stop-loss order starts with identifying the stop-loss level, which is the price at which your asset will automatically begin the selling process. This level should not be set randomly; it requires careful consideration of the asset's price history, volatility, and current market conditions. To set a stop-loss order, you first select the cryptocurrency for which you want to set the order, then choose the "stop-loss" option in the order window of your trading platform. Here, you will input the price you want the stop-loss to trigger. It is crucial to ensure that this price is set at a level that mitigates risks while providing enough room for the asset to fluctuate within normal ranges. Setting it too close to the current price can lead to the asset being sold in a brief dip, only to rise again later.

Cryptocurrency trading platforms generally provide straightforward mechanisms to implement stop-loss orders, often accompanied by tutorials or help guides to assist users in setting them up. Reviewing these resources to fully understand your chosen platform's specific steps and requirements is advisable. Additionally, many platforms allow you to set stop-loss orders as a percentage of the asset's price, which can simplify the process and ensure the order aligns with your overall risk management strategy.

Strategies for Stop-Loss Placement

Several strategies for effectively placing stop-loss orders are tailored to different trading styles and risk tolerances. A percentage-based strategy involves setting the stop-loss order at a certain percentage below the purchase price. For example, if you buy Bitcoin at $10,000, you might place a stop-loss order 10% lower, or $9,000, to limit your potential loss to 10%. This simple method can automatically adapt to the initial investment amount, making it a popular choice among new traders.

A more advanced strategy involves setting stop-loss orders based on technical analysis and market indicators. One standard method is the support level-based strategy, where stop-losses are placed just below a significant support level. This approach assumes that if the price falls below this level, it will likely continue to drop, and thus, it is a safer bet to cut losses early. Another method involves using moving averages, setting stop-loss orders at points where the price breaks below a moving average line, indicating a potential reversal in trend.

Common Mistakes in Setting Stop-Loss Orders

While stop-loss orders are a valuable risk management tool, several pitfalls can undermine their effectiveness. One common mistake is setting the stop-loss price too close to the average trading range, which can trigger the order by normal market volatility, leading to an unnecessary sale. This often happens because traders want to minimize losses, but tight stop-losses can prevent the trading strategy from reaching its potential.

Another error is failing to adjust the stop-loss order to reflect changed market conditions or new information. As the price of a cryptocurrency increases, it's prudent to move the stop-loss order up to lock in gains, a tactic known as **"trailing stop-loss."** However, this requires regular market monitoring and adjustment of the stop-loss level, which some traders neglect, leaving them vulnerable to sudden downturns after significant price increases.

Incorporating stop-loss orders into your trading strategy requires a balanced approach, careful planning, and continuous adjustment. By understanding how to set and manage these orders effectively, you can protect your investments from unexpected market movements and enhance your trading outcomes, making your venture into the volatile cryptocurrency world more secure and potentially more profitable.

2.5 Common Crypto Investment Mistakes and How to Avoid Them

Investing in cryptocurrencies can be as thrilling as rewarding, yet it's fraught with pitfalls that can challenge even the most seasoned investors. Recognizing and avoiding common mistakes is crucial to optimizing your investment outcomes.

One frequent error that many fall into is **overtrading**. This occurs when an investor makes excessive trades to capitalize on market fluctuations. While the digital currency market operates around the clock and is known for its volatility, overtrading can significicantly erode profits through fees and lead to poor decision-making. Each trade incurs a cost, and these can quickly accumulate, diminishing your overall returns. Moreover, overtrading often leads to **decision fatigue**, where the quality of your decisions degrades as you make more of them quickly. To avoid this, establish a well-thought-out trading plan with clear objectives and stick to it, resisting the urge to chase losses or react impulsively to market movements. The takeaway here is that every investment strategy benefits from consistent execution.

The crypto market is also particularly susceptible to hype and the Fear of Missing Out (FOMO) phenomenon. Social media and news platforms can amplify these effects, broadcasting an array of opinions and speculations that can lead to an emotional rollercoaster for investors. The danger here lies in making investment decisions based on what's trending rather than solid data and personal conviction. Hype can inflate the value of specific cryptocurrencies beyond their reasonable market worth, leading to unsustainable bubbles that can burst, resulting in significant losses. To combat this, conduct thorough research and maintain a disciplined investment approach. Set specific goals for each investment, and ensure your decisions are based on reliable sources and aligned with your long-term financial strategy.

Another critical area often overlooked by crypto investors is security. The decentralized nature of cryptocurrencies offers numerous benefits but also exposes investors to unique risks, such as hacking and phishing attacks. Neglecting security practices can lead to disastrous consequences, including the total loss of your investments. Protect yourself using reputable cryptocurrency wallets and exchanges, enabling two-factor authentication and strong, unique passwords for each platform. Additionally, consider storing a significant portion of your digital assets in cold storage solutions, such as hardware wallets, which are not connected to the internet and are thus less vulnerable to hacks.

Lastly, inadequate research can significantly jeopardize your investment outcomes. The crypto market is complex and continuously evolving, with new projects and coins emerging rapidly. Investing based on incomplete information, or "going in blind," can lead to poor investment choices. Before investing, take the time to understand the fundamental value and innovation behind each cryptocurrency. Look into the team behind the project, the problem it aims to solve, its technology, market potential, and competitive landscape. This level of diligence helps make more informed decisions and distinguishes genuine opportunities from potential scams or underperforming projects.

In conclusion, while the cryptocurrency market offers significant opportunities for growth, it also requires careful navigation to avoid common pitfalls. By understanding and addressing these risks—through disciplined trading, skepticism towards hype, rigorous security measures, and thorough research—you can enhance your ability to make informed decisions and increase the likelihood of achieving your investment goals. Remember, successful crypto investing is not just about choosing the right assets but also about avoiding mistakes that can undermine your investment efforts.

2.6 Managing Your Investment Portfolio During Market Volatility

Market volatility is an inherent characteristic of all investments, particularly in cryptocurrency. Prices often experience sharp fluctuations based on various factors, ranging from global economic indicators and regulatory news to changes in market sentiment and technological advancements. Understanding the nature of this volatility is not just about recognizing the factors that cause price swings but also about grasping the frequency and magnitude of these movements. Volatility can present both opportunities and risks; the key is managing your investments to maximize your potential gains while minimizing possible losses.

One of the most effective strategies for navigating a volatile market is **position sizing**. This approach involves adjusting the amount of capital allocated to each investment based on your risk tolerance and the asset's volatility. For instance, you may allocate a smaller portion of your portfolio to high-volatility cryptocurrencies to mitigate potential price fluctuations. Additionally, dollar-cost averaging, as previously mentioned, is another valuable strategy. By systematically investing fixed amounts over regular intervals, regardless of market conditions, dollar-cost averaging helps smooth out the impact of volatility. This approach spreads the purchase price over time, reducing the risk associated with market timing and ensuring a consistent investment cost basis.

Having a well-thought-out exit strategy is also crucial. This means knowing when and how to exit a position, whether taking profits or cutting losses. Setting predefined criteria based on specific financial goals and market conditions can help you make rational decisions during turbulent market phases and avoid emotional transactions. For example, you might sell a portion of your holdings after the investment has achieved a specific percentage gain or sell if the market drops below a particular threshold. The decision regarding your exit strategy should be anchored in your risk appetite, ensuring that it aligns with your financial objectives and tolerance for market fluctuations.

The psychological aspect of dealing with market volatility cannot be understated. The rapid ups and downs of the cryptocurrency market can evoke strong emotional responses, leading to impulsive decisions and potential financial missteps. Maintaining a calm and disciplined approach is essential. This involves sticking to your investment plan and avoiding reactive decisions based on short-term market movements. Regularly reviewing and adjusting your investment strategy methodically can help you manage emotional responses to market fluctuations.

Tools for Monitoring Market Trends

Staying informed about market trends and movements is crucial to effectively managing your cryptocurrency portfolio. Several tools and resources can assist you in this task, providing comprehensive data and insights that can aid in making informed investment decisions. Cryptocurrency market aggregators like CoinMarketCap and CoinGecko offer a broad overview of market cap, price movements, volume, and supply data across various cryptocurrencies. These platforms also feature charts and tools for historical price comparisons and market analysis.

For more granular insights, crypto analytics platforms such as Messari provide in-depth data, including transaction analysis, regulatory developments, and blockchain activity. These tools can help identify market trends, giving you an edge in your investment strategy. Additionally, sentiment analysis tools can gauge the market's mood by analyzing social media posts and news articles, offering clues about potential market movements based on public sentiment.

Subscribing to professional news outlets and market analyses can also provide valuable information that impacts investment decisions. These sources often offer expert opinions and analyses that can help predict market trends and provide a better understanding of the complex dynamics at play. Several free resources also offer news and analysis, but careful consideration must be taken to ensure the information from these sources is unbiased and independent of authors' affiliations or interests.

Incorporating these tools into your investment strategy monitoring lets you stay ahead of trends, better understand market movements, and make more informed decisions. However, using these tools as part of a broader strategy that includes a thorough understanding of market fundamentals and personal investment goals is essential.

In summary, managing your investment portfolio during market volatility involves understanding the nature of cryptocurrency fluctuations, employing strategies like position sizing and dollar-cost averaging, and maintaining a disciplined approach to decision-making. Utilizing various tools to monitor market trends can also provide valuable insights, helping you navigate the cryptocurrency market's complexities. As we move forward, the ability to adapt to rapidly changing market conditions while adhering to a well-defined investment strategy will continue to be critical for achieving long-term financial success. This foundational understanding sets the stage for further exploration into advanced investment techniques, which will be covered in the following chapter, enhancing your ability to engage with more sophisticated investment opportunities within the crypto space.

2.7 Knowledge Check: Test Your Understanding

What is the primary goal of a buy-and-hold investment strategy in cryptocurrency?

a) To capitalize on short-term market fluctuations

b) To hold onto for several years or decades, focusing on potential long-term gains

c) To make quick profits by buying and selling frequently

d) To avoid all risks associated with the cryptocurrency market

Which of the following is NOT a vital characteristic of a short-term investment strategy in the cryptocurrency market?

a) Frequent buying and selling over short periods

b) Focus on quick returns from market volatility

c) Minimal daily time and energy investment

d) Higher exposure to transaction fees and short-term capital gains taxes

Answers:

1 – b) To hold onto for several years or decades, focusing on potential long-term gains

2 – c) Minimal daily time and energy investment

ADVANCED INVESTING TECHNIQUES

With a robust understanding of basic investment strategies and risk management, let's delve into advanced techniques to further enrich your cryptocurrency investment portfolio. Successful investors react to market movements and anticipate them, utilizing cutting-edge technologies and methodologies to capitalize on opportunities. Among these, algorithmic trading is a potent tool that harnesses automation's speed and efficiency to execute sophisticated trading strategies. While algorithmic trading may seem like an advanced topic, introducing it here is essential for comprehensively understanding the range of strategies available, even for novice investors.

3.1 Algorithmic Trading in Crypto: An Introduction

At its core, algorithmic trading in cryptocurrency involves computer programs designed to execute trades at high speed and volume based on predefined criteria. These automated systems decide to buy or sell cryptocurrency in a fraction of a second, based on signals derived from technical analysis indicators, market data, and potentially other sources such as economic indicators or news-based events.

The allure of algorithmic trading lies in its capacity to process vast amounts of data at speeds no human trader can match. It eliminates the emotional component often associated with trading decisions, adhering strictly to the pre-programmed strategy or rules. This systematic approach can lead to more consistent and potentially more profitable outcomes, as the algorithms can detect opportunities and react instantaneously, 24/7, to changes in the market—something precious in the crypto market, which never sleeps.

Benefits of Algorithmic Trading

One of algorithmic trading's primary advantages is its speed. Algorithms' ability to scan multiple markets and execute orders within milliseconds can capture opportunities that would be impossible for human traders. Additionally, these systems can simultaneously monitor and trade across various cryptocurrency exchanges and market conditions, maximizing coverage and increasing the profit potential.

Accuracy is another significant benefit. Algorithmic trading minimizes the risk of human error and ensures that trades are executed precisely at the desired levels, adhering strictly to the predetermined strategy. Furthermore, the capability to backtest strategies against historical market data is invaluable. It allows traders to refine and adjust their approaches based on comprehensive feedback, enhancing their effectiveness before deploying them in live markets.

Types of Algorithms Used in Cryptocurrency Investing

- **Arbitrage algorithms** aim to exploit price discrepancies across different exchanges. For example, if Bitcoin sells for $20,000 on one exchange and $20,050 on another, an arbitrage algorithm would buy it at the lower price and sell it at the higher price, capturing the $50 difference as profit.

- **Trend-following algorithms** are designed to identify and follow established market trends. They might use indicators such as moving averages or momentum oscillators to signal buys or sells based on the direction and strength of market price trends.

- **Market-making algorithms** facilitate trading by continuously buying and selling cryptocurrencies at favorable prices. They profit from the spread between the buying and selling prices while providing liquidity to the market.

Getting Started with Algorithmic Trading

Embarking on algorithmic trading requires careful preparation and understanding of the technology and the market. First, you'll need to choose the right software and hardware. Many platforms cater to algorithmic traders, offering varying complexity and customization. The choice of platform should align with your technical expertise and trading needs. Starting with demo accounts provided by many platforms is advisable to familiarize yourself with the system without financial risk.

Choosing the right trading platform is crucial—look for platforms that support algorithmic trading with robust security features, high reliability, and low latency. Additionally, learning the basics of writing a trading algorithm is essential. This might involve understanding programming languages commonly used in trading software, such as Python. Numerous online courses and resources can provide the foundational knowledge to develop trading algorithms.

Algorithmic trading in cryptocurrency represents an advanced technique that offers significant advantages but requires a deep understanding and technical proficiency. While algorithmic systems' speed, accuracy, and potential profitability can be compelling, it's crucial to recognize that these tools are unsuitable for all investors. They require a comprehensive grasp of programming, market dynamics, and risk management strategies. Moreover, algorithmic trading operates in a highly competitive environment where institutional investors and sophisticated traders dominate. Nevertheless, gaining insights into algorithmic trading enhances your understanding of market participants and their strategies. This knowledge can be invaluable, even if you choose not to engage directly in algorithmic trading, as it provides a deeper comprehension of the evolving dynamics within the cryptocurrency market.

3.2 Leveraging DeFi for High Returns: Opportunities and Risks

Decentralized Finance, or DeFi, represents a radical shift in how we can manage and invest our finances, bypassing traditional financial intermediaries like banks and brokerages. At its core, DeFi leverages blockchain technology, predominantly Ethereum, to operate financial services such as borrowing, lending, and trading on a decentralized network. This fundamental shift is not just about moving services online—it's about redefining them in an open, transparent, and accessible way, where users maintain control over their assets and interact through peer-to-peer financial networks.

DeFi extends beyond simple transactions; it includes complex financial use cases like yield farming, liquidity mining, and staking. **Yield farming**, for instance, involves lending or staking cryptocurrency in exchange for interest or fees in return. At the same time, **liquidity mining** refers to providing liquidity to a DeFi protocol and earning rewards in return. **Staking**, a slightly less complex process, involves holding funds in a cryptocurrency wallet to support the operations of a blockchain network. These mechanisms offer attractive returns that often exceed those of traditional financial products, drawing retail and institutional investors into the DeFi space. The high return potential is primarily driven by the significant demand for decentralized borrowing and lending services and the incentives provided to liquidity providers. We will dive deeper into these concepts in the upcoming staking and yield farming section.

However, with high returns come high risks. The DeFi space, while innovative and promising, is fraught with challenges. One of the primary risks involves intelligent contract vulnerabilities. Since DeFi applications are built on smart contracts that automatically execute transactions when certain conditions are met, attackers can exploit any flaw in the contract's code, potentially leading to significant losses. The infamous Decentralized Autonomous Organization (DAO) attack, where millions of dollars in Ethereum were stolen due to a brilliant contract bug, is a stark reminder of this risk.

Another prevalent issue in DeFi is impermanent loss, which occurs in liquidity pools. When you provide liquidity to a pool, and the price of your deposited assets changes compared to when they were deposited, the value of your share of the pool becomes less than if you had held onto the assets. This kind of loss becomes permanent if you decide to withdraw your liquidity at this devalued state. Furthermore, liquidity issues can arise, particularly in smaller or newer DeFi projects, where there might not be enough activity or backing, increasing the risk if significant assets are withdrawn. This underscores the importance of understanding the assets in which you intend to invest, including their fundamental characteristics, such as market capitalization and liquidity dynamics.

Several best practices should be adopted to navigate the lucrative yet risky waters of DeFi. Diversification remains a key strategy; do not allocate all your resources to a single project or type of DeFi application. Spreading your investments can help mitigate risks across different platforms and services. Continuous monitoring of your assets is also crucial. DeFi environments are dynamic and can change rapidly. Keeping a close eye on market developments, technological updates, or changes in protocol terms can inform your decisions on whether to stay or exit a position.

Furthermore, a deep understanding of the underlying protocols and technology cannot be overstated. Before investing, take the time to research how the protocols work, the security measures in place, and the project's history and development team. This knowledge base can significantly reduce the chances of falling into traps or investing in low-quality projects.

In essence, while DeFi opens up a world of opportunities for earning above-average returns, it requires a proactive approach to risk management and a solid understanding of the technology and operations of protocols. By following these best practices and staying informed, you can position yourself to take advantage of what DeFi has to offer while minimizing your exposure to potential downsides. As the DeFi sector evolves, staying educated and agile will be essential to navigate this promising yet complex landscape effectively.

3.3 Crypto Futures and Options: A Beginner's Guide

Navigating the complex world of cryptocurrency investing introduces various financial instruments that can be pivotal in managing investment risks and capitalizing on market opportunities. Crypto futures and options stand out for their strategic utility in hedging against price volatility or speculating on future movements of digital assets. Understanding these instruments, their functionalities, and how they can be integrated into your investment strategy is essential for anyone looking to deepen their involvement in the financial dynamics of cryptocurrencies.

Futures and options are derivative products, meaning their value is derived from the performance of an underlying asset, which, in this case, is a cryptocurrency like Bitcoin or Ethereum. A futures contract is an agreement to buy or sell a particular cryptocurrency at a predetermined price at a specified time. Unlike directly purchasing cryptocurrencies, which require immediate settlement, futures allow you to speculate on the asset's future price without holding it. This setup can be particularly appealing in volatile markets like crypto, where futures can be used to hedge against potential price declines by setting a selling price in advance, which could help protect investments against unfavorable market shifts.

Options provide a similar yet distinct mechanism. They give you the right, but not the obligation, to buy (a call option) or sell (a put option) a cryptocurrency at a predetermined price (strike price) on or before a specific date (expiration date). Options are valuable because they offer flexibility: a call option allows you to profit from potential price increases while limiting losses to the premium paid, whereas a put option can protect against downside risk by enabling you to sell at a higher price than the market value. This versatility makes options attractive for hedging and speculative strategies in cryptocurrency markets.

In futures and options trading, leverage plays a crucial role. Leverage allows traders to control a larger position in the market with a smaller amount of capital. For example, a 10:1 leverage ratio means you can control 10 dollars' worth of cryptocurrency for every dollar you invest. While leverage can amplify profits, it also amplifies losses. Losses can exceed your initial investment if the market moves against your position, leading to significant financial risk. Therefore, understanding leverage and its implications is essential for any trader engaging in futures and options trading, as it can magnify gains and losses based on market movements.

3.4 Staking and Yield Farming: Passive Income with Crypto

What is Staking

In the expansive landscape of cryptocurrency, staking emerges as a compelling strategy for earning passive income while contributing to the stability and security of a blockchain network. Staking involves holding a certain amount of cryptocurrency in a digital wallet to support the operations of a blockchain network. This process is crucial for networks that utilize the proof of stake (PoS) consensus mechanism, a more energy-efficient alternative to the proof of work (PoW) system used by networks like Bitcoin.

Here's how it works: in PoS, the blockchain network achieves consensus about the current state of the ledger through staking. Cryptocurrency holders who choose to stake their assets are essentially locking up their coins to be randomly selected by the network to create a new block. In return for their commitment and contribution to network health, stakers are typically rewarded with additional coins from the network, proportional to the amount they stake. This reward system not only incentivizes the maintenance and security of the blockchain but also offers stakers a way to increase their holdings without the need for energy-intensive mining.

The appeal of staking lies in its dual benefits—supporting the blockchain ecosystem while generating a stream of passive income. However, potential stakers should be aware of the risks involved, including the volatility of cryptocurrency prices and the potential for security issues in the staking platform or network. Moreover, staked assets are usually locked up for a fixed period, during which they cannot be sold or exchanged, potentially exposing the holder to losses if the market value of the staked coin drops significantly during this period.

Introduction to Yield Farming

While staking is a relatively straightforward method of earning rewards, yield farming offers a more complex but potentially more lucrative avenue for generating income within the DeFi space. Yield farming involves lending cryptocurrency assets to others through the magic of intelligent contracts and earning interest or other rewards in return. These rewards often come in the form of additional cryptocurrency tokens.

The process typically involves liquidity providers (LPs) adding their crypto assets to a liquidity pool. These pools power a marketplace where users can borrow or exchange tokens. Using algorithms, the pool automatically rebalances, holding onto a user's funds and shifting them around as necessary to ensure liquidity. In return for providing their assets to the pool, LPs receive dynamic fees derived from the underlying DeFi platform's operations. The potential returns from yield farming can be significantly higher than those from traditional staking due to the compounding of interest and fees from multiple DeFi platforms.

However, yield farming is not without its risks. The complexity of the transactions and the interdependence on multiple protocols and platforms can expose liquidity providers to higher risks, including impermanent loss, where the price of their deposited assets changes compared to when they were deposited, resulting in potential loss compared to simply holding the assets. Moreover, the intelligent contracts themselves can be vulnerable, adding a layer of risk that requires vigilance and a deep understanding of the underlying protocols.

Calculating Returns and Risks

Understanding the potential returns from staking and yield farming requires carefully analyzing several factors. For staking, the **return on investment** (ROI) primarily depends on the network's interest rate, the amount staked, and the currency's inflation rate. Calculating these returns involves assessing the **annual percentage yield** (APY), which considers the compounding frequency of rewards. For instance, if you stake 100 tokens in a network with a 10% APY, you could earn ten tokens annually, assuming no network conditions or value changes.

Yield farming returns can be trickier due to the varying interest rates and additional token rewards that can change based on the protocol and market conditions. Tools and calculators allow farmers to estimate their potential earnings based on current data. However, participants must consider the risks of cryptocurrency volatility, potential regulation changes, and liquidity issues, which can dramatically affect expected returns.

Platforms and Tools for Staking and Yield Farming

Numerous platforms and tools can facilitate staking or yield farming for those interested. Popular choices for staking include Binance, Coinbase, and Kraken, which offer built-in staking services for various cryptocurrencies with different staking rewards and conditions. These platforms provide a user-friendly interface for average users who may not be profoundly technical but wish to participate in staking.

For yield farming, platforms like Uniswap, Aave, and Compound are at the forefront, offering automated yield farming tools that help users navigate the complexities of DeFi. These platforms facilitate adding assets to liquidity pools, tracking reward rates, and reallocating assets as necessary to optimize returns. Additionally, dashboard tools like Zapper and Zerion allow yield farmers to manage and track their investments across multiple DeFi platforms, providing a consolidated view of assets and returns.

In conclusion, while staking and yield farming offer substantial opportunities for earning passive income while holding crypto, they require a responsible approach considering the inherent risks and complexities. By leveraging the right platforms and tools and maintaining a vigilant watch over market conditions and technological developments, you can strategically enhance your investment portfolio through these advanced crypto investment techniques.

3.5 ICOs, STOs, and IEOs: Investing in Crypto Offerings

In the evolving tapestry of cryptocurrency investment opportunities, Initial Coin Offerings (ICOs), Security Token Offerings (STOs), and Initial Exchange Offerings (IEOs) represent significant but distinct avenues for funding and investment. Each method has reshaped how projects raise capital and how investors can participate in the growth potential of new technologies and businesses within the blockchain ecosystem. Understanding the nuances and distinctions between these offerings is crucial for anyone looking to diversify their investment portfolio in cryptocurrencies.

ICOs, the earliest form of these fundraising mechanisms, allow startups to raise capital by issuing digital tokens in exchange for more established cryptocurrencies like Bitcoin or Ethereum. This method became wildly popular in 2017 and 2018, providing a fast route to funding without the stringent regulatory compliances typical of traditional fundraising methods. However, the lack of regulation also led to high-profile scams and projects that failed to deliver on their promises, resulting in significant investor losses.

STOs emerged as a response to the regulatory issues surrounding ICOs. These offerings are similar to ICOs but involve the issuance of security tokens that represent an investment contract into an underlying investment asset, such as stocks, bonds, funds, or real estate. STOs are subject to securities regulations, which help provide investor protection, adding a layer of security but also increasing the complexity and cost of compliance.

IEOs represent a further evolution, where token offerings are conducted on a cryptocurrency exchange platform. Exchanges that conduct IEOs perform due diligence on the projects and typically have criteria they must meet before their tokens are sold and listed. This vetting process provides additional security and credibility, benefiting projects seeking funding and investors looking for more reliability.

While the potential financial gains from these offerings can be substantial, given the early entry into fast-growing projects they might represent, they also come with significant risks. The foremost is the volatility and speculative nature of many projects. The value of tokens can be highly unpredictable, and many projects may not succeed, leading to potential and sometimes complete losses. Additionally, regulatory changes can alter the landscape dramatically, impacting the legality or viability of the tokens you hold.

A structured approach to evaluating these offerings is essential to navigate these waters safely. First, consider the credibility of the team behind the project. A robust and transparent team with a proven track record and clear identities offers more assurance than a project shrouded in anonymity. Next, assess the viability of the project itself. Look for a clear, feasible roadmap, a niche in the market, and a model that offers realistic and sustainable returns rather than just high promises.

Furthermore, understanding the **tokenomics**—how tokens are distributed, used, and valued—is crucial. Look for offerings where the token has a well-defined role in the project's ecosystem, which can provide intrinsic value to the token beyond mere speculation. Projects that lock in token usage for particular services or utilities within their platforms tend to provide more stable and sustainable value.

Case Studies of Successful and Failed Offerings

Exploring triumphs and failures in ICOs, STOs, and IEOs provides valuable lessons. One successful example is Ethereum's ICO in 2014, which raised $18 million and has since resulted in a platform that fundamentally changed the blockchain landscape by enabling decentralized applications. On the other hand, the case of the DAO attack serves as a cautionary tale. It raised $150 million via an ICO in 2016 but was quickly hacked due to vulnerabilities in its code, leading to the loss of a significant portion of the funds.

These examples underline the dual-edged nature of crypto offerings. The potential for significant returns exists, but the risks are equally high. Investors must conduct thorough due diligence, remain vigilant about regulatory landscapes, and be prepared for the high volatility inherent in these investments. By doing so, you position yourself to make informed decisions, potentially reaping the benefits of early investment in innovative projects while mitigating the risks associated with the ever-changing world of cryptocurrency offerings.

3.6 The Role of Sentiment Analysis in Cryptocurrency Trading

In the intricate dance of cryptocurrency trading, understanding market sentiment can often be as crucial as analyzing fundamental and technical data. **Sentiment analysis**, a sophisticated tool derived from data science and psychology, involves parsing through vast amounts of data from social media, news articles, and other textual sources to gauge the public's mood towards specific cryptocurrencies. This technique is becoming increasingly vital as the sentiments and opinions shared across platforms like Twitter, Reddit, and various crypto forums can significantly influence market movements.

The relevance of sentiment analysis in cryptocurrency trading stems from its ability to provide insights that are not immediately apparent through traditional technical analysis. For instance, a sudden surge in positive sentiment around a new blockchain project might precede a substantial price increase, as enthusiastic discussions often attract more investors. Conversely, a wave of negative sentiment following a controversial development or lousy press could lead to swift declines in a cryptocurrency's price. By integrating sentiment analysis into your trading strategy, you position yourself to anticipate market movements that purely data-driven approaches might miss.

Various tools and platforms have been developed to assist traders in harnessing the power of sentiment analysis. Social media monitoring tools such as Brand24 and Mention can track mentions and measure the tone and sentiment of posts concerning specific cryptocurrencies across different social platforms. Specialized crypto-analytics platforms like The Tie use complex algorithms to analyze tweets and other social messages for sentiment, providing metrics that correlate closely with price movements. These tools can filter out the noise and offer quantifiable data critical in formulating robust trading strategies.

Integrating sentiment data into traditional trading strategies involves a balanced approach. One effective method is to use sentiment analysis alongside technical indicators as a form of confirmation. For example, suppose technical analysis suggests a bullish trend and sentiment analysis shows a significant uptick in positive sentiment. In that case, this might give you more confidence in placing a buy order. Alternatively, if sentiment analysis shows increasing negativity, it could be a signal to set tighter stop-losses or to take profits earlier than planned. The key is to use sentiment as one of several tools in your arsenal, allowing you to make more informed and nuanced trading decisions.

However, it's also essential to acknowledge the limitations and challenges associated with sentiment analysis. The primary issue is the data quality, as not all posts or comments are genuine or relevant. The proliferation of spam, bots, and deliberate misinformation campaigns can skew sentiment analysis, leading to inaccurate interpretations. Furthermore, the emotional nature of human communication means that sentiment analysis is not always straightforward. Sarcasm, ambiguity, and regional slang can all lead to misinterpretations if not handled carefully by sophisticated natural language processing algorithms.

While sentiment analysis offers valuable insights to enhance your trading strategies, it should not be used in isolation. Its effectiveness increases with other analytical tools, providing a more holistic view of the market dynamics. As with any trading tool, a critical and informed approach will serve you best, helping you to navigate the complexities of the crypto markets with greater assurance and strategic insight.

As we conclude this exploration of advanced investing techniques, it's clear that the landscape of cryptocurrency trading is both complex and rich with opportunities. Each strategy offers unique advantages and challenges, from the precision of algorithmic trading to the innovative prospects of DeFi and the nuanced insights sentiment analysis provides. The key to success lies in understanding these tools and integrating them thoughtfully into your broader investment strategy. As we move forward, the next chapter will move into the security aspects of cryptocurrency, ensuring that you are well-equipped to capitalize on opportunities and protect your digital assets against potential threats. This comprehensive approach is essential for anyone looking to thrive in the dynamic world of cryptocurrency investing.

3.7 Knowledge Check: Test Your Understanding

What is one of the advantages of algorithmic trading in the cryptocurrency market?

a) The ability to make decisions based on personal intuition

b) Elimination of the need for technical analysis

c) Execution of trades at high speed and volume with minimal human error

d) Guaranteed profits regardless of market conditions

What is a critical risk associated with participating in DeFi platforms?

a) Guaranteed low returns

b) Vulnerabilities in smart contracts that can be exploited

c) Lack of digital assets for trading

d) Inability to withdraw funds

Answers:

1 – c) Execution of trades at high speed and volume with minimal human error

2 – b) Vulnerabilities in smart contracts that can be exploited

SECURITY AND SAFEGUARDING YOUR INVESTMENTS

In a world where digital frontiers are continuously expanding, the allure of cryptocurrency investing is undeniable. Yet, the digital nature inherent to cryptocurrencies also makes them a prime target for various security threats. As an investor, understanding and implementing robust security measures is not just prudent—it's imperative. This chapter provides the best practices to fortify your digital assets against potential threats, ensuring your secure journey into cryptocurrency investing.

4.1 Best Practices for Crypto Security: Keeping Your Digital Assets Safe

The foundation of your cryptocurrency security begins with the network you use to access, trade, and manage your digital assets. Public Wi-Fi, convenient as it may be, is a hotbed for potential security breaches. These networks are often inadequately secured, offering minimal resistance against intrusions. Hackers on the same network can deploy various techniques to intercept your data, leading to compromised personal and financial information.

Instead, prioritize using secure, private networks, especially when handling transactions or accessing cryptocurrency accounts. For an added layer of security, consider using a **Virtual Private Network** (VPN). A VPN encrypts your internet connection and masks your IP address, making it considerably more difficult for third parties to track your online activities or intercept data you send and receive. This is particularly crucial when trading or managing your investments from locations where you cannot fully trust the security of the local internet connection.

Regular Software Updates

Keeping the software related to your cryptocurrency dealings up to date is crucial in safeguarding your digital assets. This includes your devices' operating system, cryptocurrency wallets, and trading apps. Developers continuously refine this software to enhance security features and fix vulnerabilities that hackers could exploit.

Each update not only enhances functionality but also fortifies security defenses, addressing any potential vulnerabilities that have been discovered since the last update. Neglecting these updates exposes you to known risks, leaving the door open for attackers. Configure your devices to receive automatic updates where possible, ensuring you're always equipped with the latest security defenses.

Multi-Signature Wallets

Multi-signature wallets offer a compelling solution for those seeking additional security for their digital assets. These wallets require multiple keys to authorize a transaction involving multiple parties or devices. The fundamental advantage here is that if one key or device is compromised, the intruders cannot access your funds, as they would need the other keys, which are not stored together and possibly require another party's authorization.

This setup is ideal for individuals seeking enhanced security and organizations that need to enforce checks and balances on asset movement. By distributing the authorization process, multi-signature wallets reduce the risk of theft and implement a collaborative approach to asset management, which can be crucial in preventing unauthorized access and ensuring transparency.

Education on Security Breaches

Understanding and learning from past security breaches is invaluable in preventing future incidents. Consider the infamous Mt. Gox incident, where a security breach led to the loss of approximately 850,000 bitcoins, profoundly impacting the cryptocurrency market and investors' trust. Analysis shows that a combination of weak network security and inadequate wallet management contributed to the breach.

From such historical examples, the critical lessons are clear: prioritize robust security practices and remain vigilant. Regular audits of security measures, continuous education on the latest security threats, and understanding the signs of potential breaches can significantly enhance your ability to protect your investments.

By internalizing these best practices and continually adapting to new security challenges, you can significantly enhance the security of your digital assets. As cryptocurrency evolves, so should your strategies for protecting your investments. Stay informed, stay secure, and ensure that your digital wealth is well-guarded against the ever-present threats of the digital world.

4.2 Understanding Crypto Wallets: Hot vs. Cold Storage

We briefly discussed storage mechanisms earlier, but in the complex landscape of cryptocurrency, understanding the nuances of wallet storage options is pivotal for both novice and seasoned investors. Essentially, there are two primary storage solutions for digital assets: hot and cold. Hot storage, or hot wallets, refers to wallets connected to the internet. These wallets provide convenience and quick access to your assets, making them ideal for everyday transactions and trading. In contrast, cold storage refers to wallets that are not connected to the internet. Often considered the safer option, cold storage is usually used for holding cryptocurrencies over a longer term, given their reduced exposure to online threats.

The main advantage of cold storage lies in its security. Since cold wallets are offline, they are inherently resistant to hacking attacks and other online vulnerabilities to which hot wallets are susceptible. This makes them an excellent choice for storing large amounts of cryptocurrencies or for any investor prioritizing security. Typically, cold storage solutions include hardware wallets like USB devices, paper wallets, or even physical mediums that store cryptocurrencies like coins or bearer items. Each device ensures that the private keys—essential for accessing your cryptocurrency—are not exposed to the internet and thus shielded from cyber-attacks and phishing scams.

On the other hand, despite their convenience, hot wallets come with added risk primarily due to their connectivity to the internet. The constant online presence means they are more susceptible to various security threats, including malware attacks, exploit kits, and remote attacks that could compromise the integrity of wallet software. To mitigate these risks, users of hot wallets must employ robust cybersecurity measures. This includes using strong, unique passwords for wallet accounts, utilizing two-factor authentication, and regularly updating wallet software to patch any security vulnerabilities promptly. Additionally, it is wise to use reputable wallet providers who implement advanced security measures and provide regular software updates.

Examples of Hot and Cold Storage Solutions

Let's consider some examples to illustrate the practical application of these storage options. Online wallets like Coinbase Wallet and blockchain.info are widely used for hot storage due to their user-friendly interfaces and integration with exchanges, facilitating easier transactions and trades. These platforms often provide additional security features such as two-factor authentication and multi-signature support, enhancing the safety of digital assets despite their online nature.

Conversely, for those opting for cold storage, hardware wallets such as Ledger Nano S and Trezor offer robust security by storing users' private keys on physical devices that remain offline except when transactions need to be signed. These wallets are designed with sophisticated security measures to prevent external tampering and are widely recommended for those holding significant amounts of cryptocurrencies. Additionally, paper wallets, another form of cold storage, provide a simple yet effective security solution. They involve printing your public and private keys on paper and storing them safely. However, care must be taken to ensure the physical security of the paper as it is susceptible to various physical dangers such as fire and water damage.

When choosing between hot and cold storage, consider your specific needs and the cryptocurrency you plan to store. Hot wallets offer functionality for active traders and those dealing with small amounts of cryptocurrencies requiring frequent access. However, for long-term investors or those holding large amounts of cryptocurrencies, the security advantages of cold storage make it a preferable option.

Understanding these differences and choosing the right type of wallet based on your individual security needs and transaction requirements is crucial. It helps safeguard your investments and ensures peace of mind, knowing your digital assets are well-protected. As the cryptocurrency landscape evolves, staying informed about the latest wallet technology and security practices will further enhance your ability to secure your investments effectively.

4.3 Recognizing and Avoiding Cryptocurrency Scams

In the dynamic and often lucrative world of cryptocurrency, the excitement and potential for significant financial gain can, unfortunately, also attract a variety of scams. These fraudulent schemes are designed to prey on the unwary and the unprepared, capitalizing on greed, hope, and a lack of understanding. Recognizing and steering clear of these scams is crucial to safeguard your investments as you delve deeper into cryptocurrency investing.

Phishing scams remain one of the most common threats in the cryptocurrency space. These scams typically involve fraudsters attempting to obtain sensitive information such as wallet keys or login credentials by masquerading as a trustworthy entity in an electronic communication. Often, you might receive an email that appears to be from a legitimate cryptocurrency exchange or wallet provider prompting you to provide personal information or click on a malicious link, which then leads to the theft of your cryptocurrencies.

Fake ICOs present another sophisticated scam. Here, scammers create a convincing facade of a startup company, complete with a slick website and detailed whitepaper. However, the project is non-existent—a mere front to collect funds from unsuspecting investors. The fraudulent operators disappear once the money is collected, leaving investors with worthless tokens.

Ponzi schemes are also prevalent in the crypto world. These schemes promise high returns on investment by paying earlier investors with the new funds generated from new investors. The setup leads to a cycle where the scheme collapses once there are no more new investors, resulting in the loss of money for later participants. Identifying such schemes often involves scrutinizing the promised returns; if they seem too good to be true, they likely are.

Pump and dump schemes are another significant threat in the cryptocurrency market. These schemes involve artificially inflating the price of a cryptocurrency through misleading statements or false information. The orchestrators, often working in coordinated groups, promote the coin aggressively to attract unsuspecting investors, causing its price to "pump" rapidly. Once the price peaks, they sell off their holdings profitably, causing the price to "dump" sharply. This sudden drop leaves investors who bought in at the inflated price with significant losses. Identifying pump-and-dump schemes requires caution and skepticism towards sudden, unexplained price surges accompanied by aggressive market-ing tactics in online forums and social media. Staying informed and conducting thorough research before investing can help mitigate the risk of falling victim to these schemes.

Red Flags and Warning Signs

Being able to identify potential scams is paramount in the cryptocurrency arena. Several red flags might indicate fraudulent activity. High returns promised with little or no risk should always be a cause for concern. Legitimate investments typically cannot guarantee returns, especially without risks. Overly aggressive marketing tactics and pushing for quick decisions also indicate a scam, as they aim to pressure you into investing without giving you time for due diligence. Remember, taking the time to research and "sleeping on it" before making investment decisions has often prevented substantial financial losses.

Lack of information about the project team or unrealistic goals within the whitepaper can be additional warning signs. Genuine projects typically have a transparent team with verifiable personal histories and realistic, achievable goals. Moreover, any communication that requests private keys or direct transfers of cryptocurrencies should be treated with the highest suspicion—no reputable company will ask for this information.

Preventive Measures

Prevention is undoubtedly better than cure when dealing with cryptocurrency scams. Thorough research into any cryptocurrency investment or project is essential. This in-cludes scrutinizing the project's whitepaper, researching the team behind the project, and checking for any community feedback or reviews. Utilizing reputable sources for cryptocurrency transactions—such as well-known and established exchanges and wal-lets—can also significantly reduce the risk of scams.

In conclusion, maintaining a healthy skepticism is essential. As the age-old adage goes, "If it sounds too good to be true, it probably is"—a principle that applies to cryptocur-rency investments as much as any other. Beware of projects offering guaranteed returns or requiring upfront investments for higher returns. Continuously educating yourself about the latest security practices and familiarizing yourself with common cryptocurren-cy scams empowers you to make safer investment choices. These vigilant practices protect your investments and create a safer and more trustworthy digital finance environment. Remember, safeguarding your digital assets begins with your awareness and diligence.

Steps to Take if Scammed

If you suspect you've been scammed, the first step is to secure your remaining assets. This involves transferring unaffected cryptocurrencies to a new, secure wallet and changing passwords for related accounts. Reporting the incident to relevant authorities, including local law enforcement and regulatory bodies such as the Securities and Exchange Commission (SEC) in the U.S. or similar organizations in other countries, is crucial. Additionally, notifying the cryptocurrency exchange or wallet service you use can help them take necessary actions to possibly halt further transactions.

Documenting all communications and transactions related to the scam can assist the investigation. This documentation should include emails, wallet addresses, transaction IDs, and any other relevant information that can be used to trace the fraudsters.

4.4 The Importance of Two-Factor Authentication and Other Security Measures

In digital finance, the security of transactional and personal data is paramount. Amidst various security measures, Two-Factor Authentication (2FA) stands out as a critical defense mechanism that fortifies account security far beyond the traditional password system. Two-factor authentication requires two verification forms before access is granted to an account. This method significantly reduces the risk of unauthorized access, even if a password is compromised, by adding a layer of security that is typically harder for intruders to bypass.

To understand the diverse landscape of 2FA, it's helpful to explore its main types: SMS-based, app-based, and hardware token-based authentication. Each method has distinct characteristics suited to different security needs and user preferences. SMS-based 2FA, one of the most common forms, involves sending a code via text message to your phone, which you enter with your password when logging in. While this method enhances security, its reliance on mobile networks can be a vulnerability—particularly if a hacker can intercept text messages or service is unavailable.

App-based 2FA offers a more secure alternative, such as Google Authenticator or Authy. These apps generate time-sensitive codes on your device, accessible only through the app, independent of mobile networks. This method protects against SMS intercept attacks and does not require a network connection to access the generated codes. However, it necessitates that the user has access to the device on which the app is installed, which can be a limitation if the device is lost or damaged.

Hardware tokens for 2FA provide perhaps the highest security level. These physical devices generate codes at the push of a button and are immune to the most common hacking tactics since they do not rely on software or network connectivity. The downside is their cost and the inconvenience of carrying an additional device, which could be lost or stolen, denying the user access.

Implementing 2FA on platforms and wallets for cryptocurrency transactions usually involves a straightforward process. Most services provide an option to enable 2FA in your account's security settings. For app-based 2FA, this typically involves scanning a QR code with your authentication app, which then syncs the app with your account. SMS-based 2FA involves verifying your phone number through a text code. Once set up, you'll be prompted to enter the second form of authentication every time you access your account, significantly enhancing your security profile.

Beyond 2FA, other advanced security practices are crucial in safeguarding your digital assets. Biometric security, including fingerprint scanners, facial recognition, or iris scanning, adds a layer of security uniquely tied to your physical being, making unauthorized access exceedingly tricky. Behavioral biometrics is an emerging field that adds further sophistication by analyzing patterns in user activity to detect anomalies that may indicate fraudulent attempts to access the system.

Moreover, the foundation of all security measures lies in the strength and uniqueness of your passwords. Each account should have a robust and unique password, ideally generated by a password manager, to ensure complexity and avoid reuse across multiple sites. These managers can also store your passwords securely, reducing the risk of forgetting them and making it easier to manage multiple accounts.

Integrating these advanced security measures, particularly 2FA, into your digital security strategy protects your assets and contributes to the overall security and integrity of the broader cryptocurrency ecosystem. As technologies evolve and cyber threats become more sophisticated, staying informed and proactive in implementing security best practices is your best defense in the digital age.

4.5 Backup and Recovery Solutions for Your Crypto Assets

In cryptocurrency, where digital assets represent monetary value and a personal commitment to a burgeoning financial paradigm, robust backup and recovery strategies cannot be overstated. Consider your digital assets as you would any valuable property—securing them against potential threats not only from cyber-attacks but also from physical hardware failures, human error, or theft. Regular backups are a critical fail-safe, ensuring your digital investments remain retrievable and intact regardless of unforeseen adversities.

Backing up your cryptocurrency involves creating duplicate copies of your private keys—the crucial data used to authorize outgoing transactions on the blockchain and access your funds. These keys are stored in your wallet; losing them would equate to losing your assets irretrievably. Diverse methods of backup can be employed to mitigate such a catastrophic loss. Cloud storage solutions offer one convenient option, allowing you to store your encrypted backup files online, accessed from any device connected to the internet. Services like Google Drive or Dropbox provide easy-to-use interfaces and robust security measures to protect your data. However, relying solely on cloud solutions carries risks, primarily because your data is stored on servers over which you have limited control, potentially exposing it to vulnerabilities from third-party access or system failures.

An alternative or complementary method involves using external drives—such as USB drives or hard disks—as offline backup storage. These devices can be encrypted and stored in secure, geographically diverse locations to protect against theft, natural disasters, or other local adversities. While this method reduces reliance on third-party services, it requires careful physical management of the storage devices, including protection against damage or hardware degradation over time.

Physical copies, such as printed paper wallets, represent another backup security layer. Printing out your public and private keys and storing them safely or securely creates a non-digital backup immune to cyber-attacks and system failures. However, paper can degrade or be destroyed, requiring careful preservation. Ideally, a combination of these methods should be used to ensure redundancy and enhance the overall security of your backup strategy.

Encrypting your backups adds a layer of security that protects your data if your physical or digital storage mediums are compromised. **Encryption** transforms the readable data—your private keys—into a coded form that can only be decoded with the correct encryption key, typically a password or passphrase only you know. This means that even if someone were to gain unauthorized access to your backup, the encrypted data would remain secure and inaccessible without the encryption key.

Testing the recovery process is an often overlooked but essential aspect of a comprehensive backup strategy. Regular testing ensures that your backup files can be successfully decrypted and that the restored wallets are functional and accurate. This process should be conducted routinely whenever backup systems are updated or changed. Testing not only verifies the integrity of the backup but also familiarizes you with the recovery process, which can be crucial in high-stress scenarios where quick access to your funds is necessary.

Implementing a rigorous backup and recovery protocol is paramount in safeguarding your investments in the volatile world of cryptocurrency. By diversifying your backup methods, encrypting backup data, and regularly testing recovery procedures, you create a resilient security framework that protects your digital assets against various risks. This proactive approach secures your financial investments and provides peace of mind, knowing that your digital wealth is well-protected and recoverable, come what may.

4.6 Security Myths Debunked: What You Need to Know About Crypto Security

In the ever-evolving landscape of cryptocurrency, misconceptions about security can often mislead or unnecessarily concern investors. Addressing these myths is crucial for a more precise understanding and better security practices. By debunking these misconceptions, we aim to clarify effective security measures in the digital asset space. Let's explore some of the most pervasive myths and misconceptions.

One prevalent myth is the belief that all cryptocurrencies provide complete anonymity. Most cryptocurrencies, including Bitcoin, are pseudonymous, not anonymous. This means that while the user's identity is not directly tied to their cryptocurrency wallet, their transaction history is publicly recorded on the blockchain. This public ledger allows wallet addresses to be linked to individuals through sophisticated data analysis or through the trail of transactions that interact with regulated exchanges. The pseudonymous nature of these transactions emphasizes the need for privacy-enhanced measures if anonymity is a goal, but it also highlights the importance of security. Understanding the transparency of blockchain can encourage you to be more cautious about how and where you transact, enhancing your operational security.

Another widespread belief is that blockchain technology is entirely unhackable. While blockchain's decentralized nature and cryptographic foundation make it exceptionally secure, it's not infallible. The technology might have robust security, but other components like cryptocurrency exchanges, wallet software, and user interfaces can introduce vulnerabilities. These platforms and tools, which help users interact with the blockchain, can be susceptible to cyber-attacks. For instance, exchange platforms have been frequent targets, experiencing breaches resulting in the loss of millions in cryptocurrency. It's critical to differentiate between the security of blockchain technology and the security practices of platforms that interact with it. This understanding should encourage you to use highly reputable exchanges and wallets that actively invest in security measures and to stay updated on the latest security practices.

Addressing the myth that all wallets offer equal security is also essential. The truth is that the security level varies significantly between different types of wallets. For example, hardware wallets, which store users' private keys offline on a physical device, offer enhanced security by being less vulnerable to online hacking attempts than software wallets connected to the internet. Even among hardware and software wallets, features like encryption strength, the ability to update firmware, and the quality of user interface can vary, affecting the overall security. When choosing a wallet, it's crucial to consider these factors, understanding that paying more for a reputable hardware wallet might provide significant security benefits over a free software wallet.

Finally, there's a common misconception that small investments do not require stringent security measures. This notion can lead to lax security practices, making even small holdings an easy target for thieves. The reality is that good security practices are essential regardless of investment size. Adopting robust security measures from the start protects your current assets, irrespective of their size, and prepares you to manage more significant investments as your portfolio grows securely. It's about cultivating habits that scale with your investment activities, ensuring long-term security and peace of mind.

Recognizing and understanding these myths helps clarify what you can do to enhance your security and encourages a proactive approach to managing your digital assets. As you continue to navigate the complexities of cryptocurrency investing, keep these debunked myths in mind. They serve as a reminder that knowledge truly is power in the world of crypto—the power to protect your investments effectively and to navigate the crypto space with increased confidence.

As this chapter concludes, we've tackled some of the most common security myths, providing a more transparent, more accurate picture of what to expect and how to behave in cryptocurrency. Remember, the key to robust crypto security lies in understanding the technologies and recognizing the nuances of how they're implemented and interacted with. As we move forward, the next chapter will explore legal considerations in cryptocurrency, an area just as pivotal to your investment journey. Here, you'll learn about the regulatory landscapes shaping how crypto operates globally, ensuring that your investments comply with the evolving tapestry of international laws.

4.7 Knowledge Check: Test Your Understanding

What is a critical security practice when accessing your cryptocurrency accounts to prevent unauthorized access?

a) Using public Wi-Fi for convenience

b) Only trading cryptocurrencies during peak hours

c) Utilizing secure, private networks and considering a VPN

d) Disabling two-factor authentication for ease of access

What is a significant advantage of using cold storage for cryptocurrency?

a) Faster access to funds for daily transactions

b) Enhanced security due to being offline and less vulnerable to hacking

c) Ability to earn interest on stored cryptocurrencies

d) Compatibility with all cryptocurrency exchanges

Answers:

1 – c) Utilizing secure, private networks and considering a VPN

2 – b) Enhanced security due to being offline and less vulnerable to hacking

Make a Difference with Your Review

Unlock the Power of Generosity

"The best way to find yourself is to lose yourself in the service of others."
- Mahatma Gandhi

Did you know that doing something nice for someone else can make you happier, live longer, and even help you make more money? Well, it's true! And I believe we can make that happen together right now.

I have a small favor to ask you…

Would you be willing to help someone you've never met, even if you don't get any credit for it?

Who is this person, you might ask? They're just like you but might be new to cryptocurrency, eager to learn, and looking for guidance.

My mission is to make learning about cryptocurrency simple and fun for everyone. I help people understand Bitcoin, avoid mistakes, and start making money, even if they're just beginners. But to reach as many people as possible, I need your help.

Most people do judge a book by its cover and its reviews. So here's what I'm asking for the sake of a new learner out there:

Please help them by leaving a review for this book.

Your kind words will cost you nothing and will only take about 60 seconds to write, but they can make a huge difference in someone's life. Your review could help…

- …one more person understand cryptocurrency.

- …one more reader feel confident about their financial future.

- …one more individual avoid costly mistakes.

- …one more family achieve their dreams.

- …one more future investor change their life.

To get that awesome feeling of helping someone else and making a real difference, all you have to do is... leave a review. It takes less than 60 seconds!

Simply scan the QR code below to leave your review:

Thank you from the bottom of my heart. Now, let's get back to learning all about cryptocurrency!

- Your biggest fan, Jordan Taylor

PS - Fun fact: Helping someone else makes you more valuable to them. If you think this book is helpful, share it with someone you know who could use it, too!

LEGAL AND REGULATORY ENVIRONMENT

In cryptocurrency, where innovation races ahead at breakneck speed, the legal and regulatory frameworks often shuffle along, trying to keep pace. This landscape of rules and regulations, varying wildly across different countries and regions, forms a complex tapestry that any investor—novice or experienced—must navigate carefully. Understanding these regulations is not just about compliance; it's about recognizing opportunities and risks, shaping strategies, and, sometimes, steering clear of potentially dangerous legal entanglements.

5.1 Global Cryptocurrency Regulations: What Investors Need to Know

Overview of Global Regulations

The global approach to cryptocurrency regulation can appear as diverse as the cryptocurrencies themselves. In the United States, the regulatory environment is famously fragmented, with entities like the Securities and Exchange Commission (SEC), the Commodity Futures Trading Commission (CFTC), the Internal Revenue Service (IRS), and others each having a hand in how digital assets are governed. Across the Atlantic, the European Union is moving towards a more unified approach with proposals like the

Markets in Crypto-Assets (MiCA) regulation, aiming to streamline the disparate national policies into a cohesive whole.

Asia presents its patchwork of regulatory stances, with countries like Japan taking a relatively progressive stance by recognizing cryptocurrencies as legal property under the Payment Services Act. In contrast, China has taken a much harder line by banning cryptocurrency transactions altogether. Emerging markets, often seen as fertile ground for cryptocurrency adoption, fluctuate wildly in their regulatory responses—some, like El Salvador, have embraced cryptocurrencies by adopting Bitcoin as legal tender. In contrast, others have imposed strict regulations or outright bans due to concerns over volatility, control, and financial security.

Comparison of Regulatory Approaches

The dichotomy between proactive and restrictive regulatory jurisdictions provides a fascinating lens through which to view global cryptocurrency strategies. Proactive jurisdictions such as Switzerland and Singapore have established themselves as crypto havens, employing clear, supportive legislation that fosters growth and innovation in the blockchain and crypto sectors. These regions see technological advancement and economic development as paramount, and they craft their regulations to protect investors while promoting industry health.

On the flip side, restrictive jurisdictions often cite investor protection, financial security, and control of illegal activities as reasons for their stringent regulations or outright bans. Such stances can stifle the local cryptocurrency industry but are typically motivated by broader economic policies or national security concerns. The key for you, as an investor, is to understand not just the letter of these laws but also their spirit and the stability and predictability of the regulatory environment.

Impact on International Trading

The regulatory discrepancies can pose unique challenges for cryptocurrency investors engaging in or considering cross-border transactions. A transaction legal in one country can be illegal in another, potentially leading to frozen assets or legal complications. Cryptocurrencies' decentralized nature adds complexity, as traditional geographic or jurisdictional boundaries do not confine transactions. Navigating this requires a good grasp of the regulations in your home country and an understanding of the legal landscape in any other country where you might conduct transactions.

This international regulatory puzzle emphasizes the importance of due diligence and the need for sophisticated strategies that can adapt to rapidly changing regulatory environments. To navigate these complex waters effectively, it is advisable to consult with legal experts who specialize in international cryptocurrency law.

Updates and Trends in Regulation

Staying updated with the latest regulatory changes and trends is crucial in maintaining compliance and optimizing your investment strategy. The regulatory landscape constantly changes, with new guidelines, rules, and laws being proposed and implemented regularly. For instance, numerous countries' recent interest in central bank digital currencies (CBDCs) could significantly impact the regulatory frameworks surrounding cryptocurrencies.

Monitoring these changes can be daunting, but it is essential for proactive risk management. Leveraging resources such as regulatory news websites, legal advisories, and updates from financial authorities can help you stay informed. Participating in forums and discussions can provide insights and firsthand updates on how crypto community members adapt to new regulations.

Understanding these multifaceted legal frameworks equips you to comply and thrive. By examining the kaleidoscope of global regulations, you can view a spectrum of risks and opportunities, positioning yourself to capitalize on the international stage of cryptocurrency investing.

5.2 The Impact of Regulation on Cryptocurrency Markets

Regulatory announcements and changes are pivotal in shaping the cryptocurrency markets, often acting as catalysts that significantly influence market prices and investor sentiment. The nature of this impact is twofold: regulatory clarity can fuel market confidence and growth, while uncertainty or negative news can lead to volatility and sell-offs. Investors and market participants closely monitor regulatory news, knowing that new laws or regulations can affect market dynamics immediately and profoundly.

For example, when a significant economy announces positive regulation, such as legalizing cryptocurrencies, approving a more liquid fund structure, or introducing clear, supportive laws, it generally boosts market confidence. Investors feel more secure in their holdings, knowing that their investments are acknowledged by legal frameworks, reducing the risk of sudden governmental crackdowns. This security encourages more participation from retail and institutional investors, broadening the market base and increasing the overall stability of the cryptocurrency market. Conversely, announcements of restrictive regulations, such as bans on trading or stringent control measures, can cause panic and rapid sell-offs, leading investors to pull out their capital to avoid losses or legal complications. Such events underscore the market's sensitivity to regulatory climates.

Several case studies highlight the significant impact of regulatory actions on cryptocurrency markets. In 2017, when China announced a crackdown on ICOs and, later on, cryptocurrency exchanges, it led to a sharp decline in global cryptocurrency prices. The market was affected because China was a significant player in the cryptocurrency space, and the restrictive measures reduced the trading volume significantly. Another instance is the 2021 infrastructure bill in the United States, which included provisions for stricter cryptocurrency tax reporting requirements. This news initially led to market uncertainty and a drop in prices, as stakeholders worried about the implications of these requirements on trading and investment in cryptocurrencies.

Regulations also play a crucial role in bolstering investor confidence and contributing to market stability. Transparent and fair regulatory frameworks help build trust in the market, which is essential for attracting long-term investors looking for stability rather than just speculative gains. These investors are less likely to contribute to price volatility, providing a more stable market environment. Furthermore, well-regulated environments can protect investors from fraud and malpractices, which are more prevalent in unregulated or loosely regulated markets. This protection is vital for sustaining investor participation and the cryptocurrency sector's healthy growth.

However, the regulatory landscape for cryptocurrencies is still evolving, and this comes with its risks. The uncertainty of future regulations can be a significant concern for investors. Cryptocurrency markets are global, and regulatory changes in one primary market can have ripple effects worldwide. For instance, if a large economy were to impose harsh regulations or suddenly enforce stringent control over cryptocurrencies, it could lead to market instability and affect global prices. This regulatory risk requires investors to be continually informed and ready to adapt their investment strategies to mitigate potential losses.

Regulatory developments in significant economies can also indicate potential trends in other regions. For example, if regulatory authorities in the European Union adopt a favorable stance towards blockchain technology and cryptocurrencies, it could encourage other areas to consider similar approaches, aiming to attract crypto-related businesses and investments. Conversely, stringent regulations in significant markets like the United States can prompt other countries to adopt cautious stances, potentially leading to a global domino effect of restrictive measures.

Understanding these dynamics is crucial for any investor engaged in the cryptocurrency market. Staying informed about regulatory changes, interpreting their implications, and adjusting investment strategies are essential for navigating the often turbulent waters of crypto investing. Moreover, this knowledge can empower investors to advocate for fair and balanced regulations that support innovation while protecting market participants, contributing to the overall maturity and stability of the cryptocurrency ecosystem.

5.3 Understanding Know Your Customer and Anti-Money Laundering in Crypto

In the bustling world of cryptocurrency, where the excitement of innovation intersects with the necessity of regulation, two acronyms frequently come into play: KYC and AML. These regulatory frameworks are crucial for understanding how legal compliance impacts users and platforms in cryptocurrency. KYC procedures are designed to verify customers' identities, ensuring businesses know whom they deal with. This process helps prevent identity theft, financial fraud, money laundering, and terrorist financing. AML regulations, on the other hand, involve procedures, laws, and rules to stop income generation through illegal actions, ensuring that funds being invested are not derived from or will not be used for illicit activities.

You will likely encounter KYC checks when you sign up for a cryptocurrency exchange or choose a digital wallet. Typically, these involve submitting personal identification documents, such as a passport or driver's license, and sometimes proof of address through utility bills or bank statements. More advanced KYC procedures might also include biometric verification, such as facial recognition or fingerprint scans, further enhancing the security and integrity of the process. While this might seem cumbersome or even intrusive for the investor, these steps are essential for platforms to comply with regulatory requirements and ensure the ecosystem remains secure and trustworthy.

The balance between regulatory compliance and privacy is a delicate dance in crypto. On the one hand, KYC and AML protocols are fundamental in making the cryptocurrency space safer and more reliable, setting a standard that discourages illegal activities. On the other hand, these measures can raise privacy concerns, especially considering the decentralized ethos that underpins much of the cryptocurrency community. Many users are drawn to crypto because of its anonymity and autonomy, which are far removed from the often watchful eyes of traditional financial institutions. To navigate this, it's crucial for you as an investor to choose platforms that comply with KYC and AML regulations and respect and protect user data. Ensuring that a platform uses encrypted data storage, secure communication channels, and transparent privacy policies can help maintain your security.

Globally, the standards and practices for KYC and AML in the crypto sector are influenced heavily by recommendations from the Financial Action Task Force (FATF), an intergovernmental organization founded to develop policies to combat money laundering. The FATF has been pivotal in shaping the worldwide regulations that affect cryptocurrency markets, advocating for a balanced approach that ensures security without stifling innovation. Their guidelines suggest that virtual asset service providers, including crypto exchanges, should be held to the same regulatory standards as traditional financial institutions. This global framework helps harmonize the approaches taken by different countries, providing a more consistent regulatory environment that can aid in international cooperation and enforcement.

Understanding these global standards and how they impact your platforms is crucial. It helps you make informed decisions about where and how to invest and understand the broader implications of your participation in the global financial ecosystem. As regulations evolve, staying informed about these changes and understanding their implications can help you navigate the complexities of cryptocurrency investment more effectively. As the digital finance landscape expands, the interplay between regulation and innovation will undoubtedly become more intricate, underscoring the need for informed and proactive engagement.

5.4 Navigating Tax Implications for Cryptocurrency Investors

Navigating the tax implications of cryptocurrency transactions is one of the more complex aspects of digital currency investment. Understanding how different types of transactions are taxed is crucial for maintaining compliance and optimizing your financial strategy. Each transaction type—trading, mining, staking, or receiving cryptocurrency as payment—carries its tax considerations. The IRS treats these assets as property for trading cryptocurrencies, meaning that buying and selling digital currencies are taxable, and capital gains tax applies. Suppose you have held a cryptocurrency for over a year before selling it. In that case, you are subject to long-term capital gains tax, which generally offers a favorable rate compared to short-term capital gains tax, which applies if the asset is held for less than a year.

Mining cryptocurrencies also has tax implications. If you mine cryptocurrency, the market value of the coins mined when they are received becomes taxable income and must be reported. Additionally, you must report the transaction as a capital gain or loss if you sell these mined coins later. Staking, where investors lock up their coins to support a network and receive rewards, similarly results in taxable income equivalent to the fair market value of the received coins when they are received. Receiving cryptocurrency as payment, whether for goods, services or as salary, is treated as ordinary income according to the fair market value of the crypto at the time of receipt.

For reporting and compliance, accurate record-keeping is paramount. Exchanges often provide transaction histories and reports that detail dates, amounts, market values, and transaction fees, which can be deductible. You must track every transaction meticulously, ensuring it aligns with these records. When reporting cryptocurrency earnings, using the appropriate tax forms is essential—for instance, Form 8949 reports capital gains and losses from investment transactions, including cryptocurrencies. The total from this form is then transferred to Schedule D of your tax return. In cases where you receive cryptocurrency as income, it's reported using Schedule 1, and you must also consider self-employment tax if operating as a crypto business.

Tax planning strategies can significantly reduce your tax liabilities and enhance investment outcomes. One effective method is tax-loss harvesting, where you sell cryptocurrencies at a loss to offset the capital gains from other investments. This strategy is beneficial in the volatile crypto market, where significant price swings can provide opportunities to realize losses for tax purposes and potentially repurchase the cryptocurrency after a period to maintain market exposure. Another strategy involves structuring transactions to take advantage of lower tax rates on long-term capital gains. For instance, holding onto cryptocurrency investments for longer than a year before selling can reduce the tax you owe.

International tax considerations add a layer of complexity. You must navigate each jurisdiction's tax laws if you hold cryptocurrencies in multiple countries. Each country has its own rules regarding the taxation of digital assets, and the lack of uniform global cryptocurrency regulation can complicate compliance. For instance, some countries treat cryptocurrency as a currency, while others treat it as property, and these classifications can significantly impact your tax responsibilities. Understanding the countries' tax treaties can help mitigate the risk of double taxation. Working with tax professionals who are well-versed in international cryptocurrency regulations is often advisable to ensure compliance across different jurisdictions.

These tax considerations underscore the importance of staying informed and proactive in your cryptocurrency investments. As the regulatory landscape continues to evolve, keeping abreast of changes in tax legislation is crucial. Cryptocurrency taxation is complex and varies depending on individual circumstances and jurisdictional laws. It's crucial to clarify that this information is educational and should not be construed as tax advice. Therefore, seeking guidance from qualified tax professionals or advisors is recommended to ensure compliance and optimize investment returns. Their expertise and strategic planning can help navigate these complexities effectively, clarifying reporting requirements and potential deductions.

5.5 Recent Legal Cases in Cryptocurrency and Their Implications for Investors

Several high-profile legal cases have emerged in the rapidly evolving domain of cryptocurrencies, setting essential precedents and profoundly influencing the regulatory landscape. These cases highlight the legal complexities inherent in cryptocurrency transactions and provide critical insights into how laws shape the future of digital currencies and their use across the globe. Understanding these cases helps investors grasp the nuances of legal compliance and the ramifications for their investment strategies.

One of the landmark cases in the cryptocurrency space involved the SEC against Kik Interactive Inc. In this significant legal battle, the SEC alleged that Kik's sale of $100 million in digital tokens was essentially an unregistered securities offering. The court's decision favoring the SEC sent ripples through the cryptocurrency community, underscoring the potential for similar tokens to be classified as securities rather than mere currencies or utilities. This classification has profound implications for token issuers who now navigate securities laws, potentially facing stricter regulations and compliance requirements. For investors, this case highlighted the importance of assessing the legal frameworks surrounding token offerings to mitigate the risks of regulatory actions.

Another pivotal case is the ongoing saga of Ripple Labs Inc., which faces a lawsuit from the SEC alleging that its XRP token constitutes an unregistered security. This case is particularly noteworthy due to Ripple's prominence in cryptocurrency and the substantial market activity surrounding XRP. The outcome of this litigation could set a precedent for how other cryptocurrencies are viewed and regulated by authorities in the United States and internationally. For you as an investor, the implications are significant; a ruling against Ripple could affirm the need for compliance with securities laws, potentially affecting the valuation and liquidity of similar cryptocurrencies.

From these cases, several lessons emerge on navigating the legal complexities of cryptocurrency investments. First and foremost is the critical importance of understanding the legal classification of the digital tokens you invest in. Tokens classified as securities could expose issuers and investors to additional legal and regulatory scrutiny. This necessitates a thorough due diligence process to evaluate the legal standing of token offerings and the compliance measures adopted by the issuing companies. Additionally, these cases emphasize the importance of staying informed about ongoing legal developments. Regulatory landscapes can shift quickly, and being proactive in your awareness can provide a strategic advantage in managing potential legal risks.

Future legal challenges in the crypto world will likely revolve around the increasing intersection of digital currencies with mainstream financial systems and the ongoing evolution of blockchain technology. As cryptocurrencies gain wider acceptance and integrate more closely with global financial markets, they will likely attract further scrutiny from regulators and law enforcement worldwide. Issues such as consumer protection, anti-money laundering measures, and the cross-border nature of digital transactions will pose significant legal challenges. For investors, these developments necessitate a vigilant approach to compliance and a flexible investment strategy that can adapt to the changing legal environment.

Navigating this complex legal terrain requires a balanced approach, blending vigilance with proactive strategy adjustments. By keeping abreast of legal developments and understanding the implications of high-profile cases, you can better position yourself to respond to the evolving regulatory landscape, helping safeguard your investments against legal pitfalls while capitalizing on emerging opportunities.

5.6 How to Stay Compliant While Investing in Cryptocurrencies

Navigating the intricate web of compliance in cryptocurrency requires a robust understanding of the regulatory frameworks governing these digital assets. As an individual investor, it's crucial to grasp the universal aspects of these regulations and how they might impact your investment activities. Each jurisdiction has its own set of rules, ranging from broad directives issued by bodies like the European Union to localized regulations at the country or state level. Understanding these variations is essential, as non-compliance can lead to severe penalties, including hefty fines or criminal charges.

For most individual investors, compliance primarily revolves around adhering to AML and KYC regulations. These standards ensure transparency and accountability in cryptocurrency transactions. Tools and resources are available to help manage and track compliance obligations effectively. Automated compliance software tailored for cryptocurrency can streamline monitoring and reporting requirements, reducing the risk of errors.

Additionally, staying compliant requires practicing due diligence in all transactions and investments. Regular audits, both internal and external, play a crucial role in maintaining transparency and identifying any compliance gaps. Keeping abreast of the evolving regulatory landscape through education and training sessions is also vital.

In the event of compliance failures, prompt action is necessary to rectify issues and mitigate potential penalties. Legal counsel should be consulted for severe breaches to navigate regulatory complexities and ensure appropriate remedial measures.

In cryptocurrency's dynamic world, staying compliant demands vigilance and adaptability. By understanding regulatory nuances and leveraging appropriate tools, individual investors can protect their investments while operating within legal frameworks designed to safeguard the market and its participants.

As we explore the dimensions of cryptocurrency investments, the next chapter will delve into the future of digital currencies and emerging trends that shape the landscape, offering insights into aligning investment strategies with these developments.

5.7 Knowledge Check: Test Your Understanding

Which of the following best describes the global regulatory landscape for cryptocurrencies?

- a) Uniform and consistent across all countries
- b) Completely unregulated worldwide
- c) Highly fragmented and varies widely between countries
- d) Harmonized under a single international body

What is the purpose of Know Your Customer (KYC) regulations in cryptocurrency?

- a) To ensure that all cryptocurrencies are taxed equally
- b) To verify customers' identities and prevent illegal activities
- c) To control the price of cryptocurrencies
- d) To facilitate the sale of cryptocurrencies without restrictions

Answers:

- 1 – c) Highly fragmented and varies widely between countries
- 2 – b) To verify customers' identities and prevent illegal activities

THE FUTURE OF CRYPTOCURRENCY

As we stand at the cusp of a financial revolution, the ripple effects of cryptocurrency's ascent are reshaping the contours of modern finance. This chapter discusses the profound transformation ushered in by digital currencies, tracing their roots from ancient barter systems to today's sophisticated blockchain networks. It's a journey through time, highlighting how each phase of monetary evolution has set the stage for the next and, most importantly, how cryptocurrencies are poised to redefine the future of money. You will better understand the dynamic digital asset landscape by exploring these emerging trends and innovations. This knowledge will shape your perception of current financial systems and opportunities and guide your future research and investments in the ever-evolving world of cryptocurrencies.

6.1 The Evolution of Money: Cryptocurrency and the Future of Finance

Historical Context and Evolution

The story of money is as old as civilization, beginning with the barter systems of ancient societies, where goods were directly exchanged for other goods. The limitations of barter led to the creation of money as a medium of exchange, initially in the form of commodities like grains or livestock, which eventually evolved into precious metals and coins. Fast forward to the modern age, where paper currency and digital transactions have become the norm; each stage of monetary evolution has been driven by a need for greater efficiency, trust, and broader economic reach.

Cryptocurrencies enter this historical narrative as the latest iteration, emerging as a response to the Global Financial Crisis of 2008. This genesis speaks volumes about their intended purpose—to create an economic system that is transparent, decentralized, and free from the control of any single authority. Unlike traditional currencies, which governments and central banks regulate, cryptocurrencies operate on decentralized blockchain technology. This reduces the risk of manipulation and democratizes financial opportunities, allowing anyone with an internet connection to participate.

Cryptocurrencies as an Alternative Financial System

The appeal of cryptocurrencies lies in their ability to challenge the status quo of traditional banking. They offer several transformative advantages, the chief one being decentralization. Cryptocurrencies reduce transaction costs significantly by eliminating the middleman—typically banks and financial institutions. Additionally, transactions are often processed more quickly without cumbersome paperwork or extensive compliance checks, making them more accessible to the world's unbanked and underbanked populations.

Another key advantage is the inherent security offered by blockchain technology. Each transaction is recorded on a block and linked to the previous and subsequent blocks, creating a secure, unalterable chain. The encryption and distribution of data across multiple nodes ensure that hacking attempts are not only easily detectable but also highly impractical, as altering any information would require overriding the entire network.

Impact on Global Financial Systems

The widespread adoption of cryptocurrencies has the potential to alter global financial systems dramatically. For one, it could challenge the hegemony of traditional fiat currencies and reshape monetary policies. Central banks may need to adapt to a world where digital currencies dominate, possibly even incorporating blockchain technologies to issue their digital currencies.

Moreover, cryptocurrencies' global nature makes them an intriguing tool for international trade. They could reduce the need for currency exchanges, simplify cross-border transactions, and decrease the costs of international money transfers. This financial fluidity could increase global trade efficiency, potentially fostering more robust economic relationships between countries.

Future Predictions

Looking ahead, the trajectory of cryptocurrencies is likely to be influenced by various factors, from technological advancements to regulatory frameworks. One potential scenario is the mainstream adoption of cryptocurrencies as an investment asset class and a widely accepted medium for frequent transactions. Integration with existing financial technologies, like mobile payment systems, could pave the way for this transition, making digital currencies as routine as credit cards.

Moreover, the evolution of cryptocurrencies might lead to entirely new financial products and services. Imagine DeFi platforms that offer everything from insurance to loans without the need for traditional financial institutions. The vast possibilities could lead to a more inclusive economic system that empowers individuals rather than institutions.

In conclusion, as we explore the potential futures of cryptocurrency, it becomes clear that this is not just about digital money. It's about reimagining what money is and what it can do. The evolution from barter to digital currencies is not just a change in the form of cash but a revolution in financial systems architecture—a shift that could redefine global finance for generations.

6.2 Decentralized Finance: The Next Evolution in Financial Markets

In this section, we explore DeFi in more detail. DeFi, short for Decentralized Finance, represents a transformative shift in the financial sector. It leverages blockchain technology to orchestrate financial transactions without traditional intermediaries like banks, brokers, or exchanges. At its core, DeFi aims to create an open, accessible, and highly flexible financial market structure that operates independently of centralized financial powerhouses. This shift not only challenges the conventional financial ecosystem but also seeks to redefine the mechanics of financial transactions globally.

DeFi is built on a foundation of blockchain technology, primarily Ethereum, which supports the execution of complex agreements known as smart contracts. These contracts automatically execute transactions when certain conditions are met without a middleman. The architecture of DeFi is composed of several key components, each playing a pivotal role in its functionality. Smart contracts are the backbone, facilitating the creation of dApps (decentralized applications) that operate these financial transactions. Decentralized exchanges allow for the peer-to-peer exchange of cryptocurrencies without a central authority, providing a more direct and possibly more secure trading environment. Automated lending protocols offer another cornerstone of DeFi, enabling users to lend out their cryptocurrencies or take out loans, all managed automatically through smart contracts without needing a traditional credit check or intermediary.

The advantages of DeFi over traditional financial systems are compelling, particularly in terms of transparency, accessibility, and efficiency. The blockchain ledger, where all DeFi transactions are recorded, is public and immutable. This transparency ensures that any user can verify the authenticity and fairness of transactions. Accessibility is significantly enhanced in DeFi ecosystems as they are inherently designed to be inclusive, requiring only an internet connection and a digital wallet to participate. This opens up financial services to a global audience, including those in unbanked or underbanked regions who may not have access to traditional banking services. Moreover, DeFi applications can run autonomously on blockchain technology, reducing the overhead costs associated with human operators and physical infrastructure and passing on these cost savings to users through lower fees and higher interest rates on investments and savings.

Despite its potential, DeFi is not without its challenges. Scalability remains a significant concern; as more users engage with DeFi platforms, the underlying blockchain infrastructure can become congested, leading to slower transaction times and higher processing fees. Additionally, while smart contracts are robust, they are only as reliable as the code they are written with. Bugs or vulnerabilities in smart contract code can lead to security issues, potentially resulting in the loss of a substantial amount of money. Compliance with existing financial regulations is also a complex issue for DeFi. DeFi operates in a grey area of financial regulation as a new economic model, leading to uncertainties around compliance and potential legal challenges for users and developers.

DeFi's trajectory is poised to reshape the financial landscape dramatically. As blockchain technology evolves and matures, solutions to challenges such as scalability and security will likely be developed, paving the way for more robust and reliable DeFi applications. Furthermore, as regulatory bodies understand and adapt to the nuances of blockchain and DeFi, more transparent regulations could emerge, which would help integrate DeFi into the mainstream financial ecosystem more seamlessly. In addition, the continuous innovation in blockchain technology, like developing more efficient consensus mechanisms or integrating artificial intelligence, could further enhance the capabilities, efficiency, and security of DeFi systems.

In essence, as you explore the possibilities within DeFi, you are not only participating in an alternative financial system. Still, you are also at the forefront of a movement that could define the future of finance. With its promise of democratization, decentralization, and disintermediation, DeFi represents a radical departure from traditional finance that could potentially level the economic playing field globally by providing universal access to financial services. As this sector evolves, staying informed and adaptable will be vital to navigating the promising yet fluctuating landscapes of Decentralized Finance.

6.3 Non-Fungible Tokens: Understanding the Hype and Value

Non-fungible tokens (**NFTs**) have captured the public's imagination like other financial phenomena in recent history. Unlike traditional cryptocurrencies such as Bitcoin or Ethereum, which are fungible, meaning each unit is identical and interchangeable, NFTs are unique digital assets. Each NFT has distinct characteristics that set it apart from others, even those on the same platform or collection. This uniqueness is primarily due to the metadata and digital content linked to the NFT, which cannot be replicated or divided into smaller parts. This differentiation makes NFTs perfect for representing ownership of unique items, both digital and physical, thereby creating a bridge between the tangible and digital worlds.

The use cases of NFTs extend far beyond the art sector, where they first gained prominence. For example, NFTs are revolutionizing how players interact with their games in the gaming industry. They allow players to own in-game assets—from costumes to weapons—that can be traded on NFT marketplaces or transferred across different gaming platforms. This enhances the gaming experience by adding a layer of investment and ownership and creates a new revenue model for game developers.

Real estate is another sector where NFTs are making an impact. Traditionally, real estate transactions are complex, requiring multiple intermediaries, including brokers, legal teams, and banks. NFTs streamline this process by representing property ownership digitally on the blockchain. This transformation reduces transaction times, cuts costs, and enhances transparency, making real estate investment more accessible to a broader audience. Moreover, NFTs in real estate are not limited to physical properties. Virtual real estate, plots of digital land in virtual worlds and platforms, can also be bought, sold, or developed, just like physical land.

Intellectual property rights management is yet another area where NFTs offer significant advantages. Artists, musicians, authors, and other creators can use NFTs to assert ownership rights over digital creations, control the distribution, and streamline royalty payments. Each transaction or use of the NFT can be tracked, ensuring that creators receive fair compensation for their work, potentially transforming copyright management systems.

The market dynamics of NFTs are driven by their novelty and the speculative nature of their markets. The scarcity of specific NFTs, often artificially created by the issuers, can lead to significant price increases, attracting investors looking for high returns. However, the market is also characterized by high volatility and liquidity issues, as the value of NFTs is highly subjective and can fluctuate widely based on consumer perceptions and trends. While some NFTs have sold for millions, others struggle to find a market, highlighting this investment's speculative and risky nature.

The future outlook for NFTs is as diverse as their applications. Technological advancements are expected to expand the functionality and interoperability of NFTs, integrating them more seamlessly with existing digital platforms and possibly creating new forms of digital interaction and transaction. For instance, integrating NFTs with augmented reality (AR) and virtual reality (VR) technologies could enhance virtual experiences, making digital assets more tangible and valuable.

Furthermore, as the regulatory landscape around digital assets becomes more transparent and standardized, NFTs could become more integrated into traditional financial and legal systems, potentially leading to broader adoption. However, challenges such as ensuring the sustainability of NFTs, particularly concerning their environmental impact due to the energy-intensive nature of blockchain networks, need addressing. Solutions such as more energy-efficient consensus mechanisms or using carbon offsets by NFT platforms could help mitigate these issues.

In exploring NFTs, you are not just looking at a novel asset class. You are witnessing the merging of technology, finance, and creativity in ways that challenge our traditional understanding of ownership and value. As this sector evolves, it promises to redefine existing industries and create new opportunities and markets that we are just beginning to imagine.

6.4 The Integration of Cryptocurrency with Traditional Banking

The landscape of financial services is witnessing a fascinating evolution as the lines between traditional banking systems and innovative cryptocurrency technologies continue to blur. This integration, though still in its nascent stages, is driven by the mutual benefits it offers to banks and the broader blockchain ecosystem. For traditional banks, incorporating cryptocurrency can significantly enhance operational efficiencies, reduce transaction costs, and open new revenue streams. Conversely, associating with established financial institutions lends credibility to cryptocurrencies and facilitates wider user adoption.

Currently, the level of integration varies significantly from one institution to another. Some banks have started experimenting with blockchain technology to improve their operations, such as cross-border transactions and asset management, which are often cumbersome and opaque. Others have partnered with cryptocurrency platforms to offer digital asset custody services or facilitate crypto trading for their clients. These early adopters are paving the way for a more comprehensive integration, which could eventually reshape the banking industry as we know it.

However, merging traditional banking with cryptocurrency is not without its challenges. Regulatory hurdles are perhaps the most significant barrier. Cryptocurrencies' decentralized and often anonymous nature conflicts with the highly regulated banking industry, which strict KYC governs and AML guidelines. Banks must closely monitor customer activities and report suspicious transactions, a requirement that is hard to reconcile with the privacy and anonymity fundamental to many cryptocurrencies.

Technological compatibility also poses a significant challenge. Integrating blockchain technology with traditional banks' existing IT infrastructure requires substantial investment in time and resources. Additionally, the scalability issues associated with major cryptocurrencies like Bitcoin and Ethereum can limit their practical use in high-frequency banking operations. Despite these challenges, the potential benefits of integration continue to drive forward the collaboration between traditional banking and cryptocurrency sectors.

Several case studies highlight the successful integration of cryptocurrency technologies within traditional banking systems. J.P. Morgan Chase, one of the largest banking institutions in the world, launched JPM Coin, a digital token to facilitate instant payments between institutional clients. The development of JPM Coin not only streamlined payment processes but also demonstrated the potential for other banks to develop their digital currencies for various uses.

In Europe, the Swiss bank UBS led a consortium of financial institutions to create the Utility Settlement Coin (USC), a digital coin aimed at facilitating cross-border transactions among banks. The initiative is designed to reduce the time, costs, and capital required in traditional interbank settlements, highlighting a significant step towards integrating cryptocurrency technologies within established financial operations.

The relationship between traditional banks and cryptocurrency will likely grow more profoundly and become more complex. We might see increased banks offering cryptocurrency-related services, including trading, custody, and ATM offerings. This integration could extend beyond financial transactions to include blockchain solutions for various banking operations, from loan issuance and risk management to compliance and fraud prevention.

Moreover, integrating cryptocurrency technology into traditional banking could accelerate as central banks worldwide explore the possibility of issuing their digital currencies, commonly called Central Bank Digital Currencies (CBDCs). These government-issued digital currencies could operate on blockchain platforms, offering the benefits of cryptocurrencies—efficiency, transparency, and security—while retaining traditional fiat currencies' regulatory and stabilizing functions.

As banks continue to navigate the complexities of this integration, the potential for innovation and transformation in the banking sector remains vast. The convergence of traditional banking and cryptocurrency promises more efficient, secure, and inclusive financial services and signifies a shift towards a more integrated global economic system. As this integration deepens, it will likely unlock new opportunities for consumers and businesses alike, heralding a new era in the evolution of finance.

6.5 Cryptocurrency and IoT: Exploring the Convergence of Technologies

The **Internet of Things** (IoT) represents a vast network of devices communicating and operating over the Internet, from everyday household items to sophisticated industrial tools. These devices collect and exchange data, making them more innovative and responsive, transforming how we live, work, and interact with our environment. Integrating blockchain and cryptocurrency technologies with IoT devices significantly enhances these capabilities, providing a new layer of functionality and security. Blockchain technology offers a secure, immutable platform for the vast data these devices generate, while cryptocurrency automates transactions between devices with precision and transparency. This convergence amplifies the utility of IoT devices and opens up innovative avenues for data security and financial transactions, paving the way for a more interconnected and efficient digital ecosystem.

Benefits of merging IoT with cryptocurrencies

One of the most compelling benefits of integrating IoT with cryptocurrencies is the enhanced security of IoT devices. Traditional IoT systems face significant security challenges, including susceptibility to hacking and data breaches, due to the centralized nature of their data exchanges. Blockchain technology introduces decentralization into these transactions, distributing data across a network of nodes. This not only makes it incredibly difficult for any single point of attack to succeed but also ensures that any tampering with the data can be easily detected and rectified. Additionally, the cryptographic algorithms inherent to blockchain further secure the data against unauthorized access and tampering.

Privacy enhancements are another critical benefit of this integration. IoT devices often handle sensitive data, including personal information, and protecting this data is paramount. Blockchain's decentralized structure ensures that personal data can be processed and stored without revealing identifying details, enhancing user privacy. Moreover, smart contracts can automate interactions between devices without human intervention, maintaining privacy while ensuring reliability and trust in the data exchange.

The convergence also fosters new models for automation and data exchange. Smart contracts, self-executing contracts with the terms directly written into code, can automate transactions between devices based on pre-set conditions. This reduces the need for human intervention, makes processes more efficient, and opens up new models for usage-based pricing, collective data sharing, and more. For instance, IoT devices in a smart home could autonomously transact electricity with a power provider based on usage or automatically order and pay for supplies when they run low, seamlessly integrating economic transactions into the functionality of smart devices.

Real-world applications

In smart homes, IoT devices integrated with blockchain are revolutionizing how we interact with our living spaces. Smart locks can enhance security by using blockchain to verify the identity of individuals before granting access, ensuring that only authorized users can enter. Similarly, intelligent appliances can autonomously perform tasks like reordering groceries or optimizing energy use, with transactions recorded securely on a blockchain.

The supply chain industry greatly benefits from this integration. Blockchain can provide a transparent, tamper-proof ledger for tracking goods from origin to delivery, significantly reducing the possibility of fraud and ensuring all parties can trust the data shared across the network. IoT devices like GPS trackers and temperature sensors can provide real-time data to this ledger, enhancing tracking accuracy and efficiency. This improves supply chain operations and enhances compliance and quality control, as every process step is recorded and verifiable.

Healthcare is another sector where the convergence of IoT and cryptocurrencies is significantly impacted. IoT devices can monitor patient health metrics in real time and store this data on a blockchain, providing secure and immediate access to healthcare providers. This can improve the quality of care and patient outcomes by enabling more timely and informed medical decisions. Additionally, smart contracts can automatically process claims and payments between healthcare providers and insurers, reducing administrative costs and delays.

Challenges and Future Potential

Despite these advancements, the integration of IoT and cryptocurrencies faces several challenges. Scalability is a significant concern as the number of IoT devices grows exponentially, potentially overwhelming existing blockchain networks. The processing power required to handle numerous transactions between these devices can lead to congestion, slowing transactions, and increasing costs. Interoperability between different IoT devices and blockchain systems is another challenge. As the IoT ecosystem consists of various devices with varying standards and technologies, ensuring these devices can communicate and transact seamlessly on blockchain platforms is crucial for widespread adoption.

The future potential of IoT and cryptocurrency integration, however, is vast. As solutions to scalability and interoperability challenges are developed, such as through advancements in blockchain technology like sharding or the establishment of universal standards for IoT devices, the full potential of this convergence could be realized. This could lead to entirely new industries and business models, such as decentralized energy grids where individuals buy and sell energy directly from each other or global logistic networks that operate autonomously, optimizing themselves in real time. As these technologies evolve and mature, their integration will likely become more seamless, leading to a more connected, efficient, and secure world.

6.6 Predicting the Next Big Cryptocurrency: What to Watch For

In the dynamic world of cryptocurrency, identifying the next prominent innovator or market disruptor requires a keen understanding of various critical factors that signal long-term viability and success. When evaluating potential cryptocurrencies, it's essential to consider aspects such as underlying technology, the competence and experience of the team, community support, and overall market potential. These elements collectively provide a comprehensive view of a cryptocurrency's foundation and ability to withstand the complexities of the market.

The technology behind a cryptocurrency is a cornerstone of its success. It's not merely about the novelty but also the technology's practicality, scalability, and security. For instance, a new cryptocurrency that proposes solutions to blockchain's limitations, such as high energy consumption or slow transaction speeds, could be poised for significant adoption. Technologies that enhance privacy provide more efficient consensus mechanisms or better integrate with existing financial infrastructures could also drive a cryptocurrency's success.

However, technology alone isn't enough. The team behind the cryptocurrency is equally crucial. A strong group combining blockchain technology, finance, cybersecurity, and business development expertise can significantly increase the project's credibility and execution capability. Researching the team's background, track record in similar projects, and overall reputation in the tech community is essential. A team that has successfully navigated previous projects and has strong ties to leading industry players is likelier to lead a project to success.

Community support is another vital aspect. The strength and enthusiasm of the community surrounding a cryptocurrency can be a powerful driver of its adoption and value. A dedicated community helps spread the word and provides a support network for testing new ideas, reporting bugs, and improving the system. Moreover, a robust community indicates high trust and satisfaction among users, which can attract more users and investors.

The market potential is the final puzzle, encompassing cryptocurrency demand and applicability in solving real-world problems. This involves analyzing the market size, potential use cases, and economic models. A cryptocurrency that addresses a substantial market need or offers a novel solution that could disrupt traditional industries may have a higher chance of widespread adoption.

Emerging trends in cryptocurrency innovation also play a pivotal role in shaping the development of new cryptocurrencies. Privacy enhancements are increasingly crucial as users seek greater anonymity in their transactions, pushing many new projects to prioritize advanced cryptographic techniques. Energy efficiency is another critical trend, especially given the environmental concerns associated with traditional blockchain models. Projects that offer solutions for reducing the energy consumption of blockchain networks are more sustainable and more likely to gain favor from regulators and the public.

Regulatory compliance is also becoming a trend as more governments and financial bodies worldwide recognize and integrate cryptocurrencies into their legal frameworks. Cryptocurrencies that comply with these regulations from the outset may find more accessible paths to mass adoption and less resistance from traditional financial systems.

Several promising projects currently exemplify these criteria. For instance, cryptocurrencies that leverage blockchain to facilitate faster and cheaper cross-border payments are seeing increasing interest. Others integrating IoT applications for smart contracts or supply chain management are also gaining traction, indicating a broadening scope of blockchain applications.

When investing in emerging cryptocurrencies, a strategic approach involves thorough research and risk assessment. Diversifying your investment across different types of cryptocurrencies can mitigate potential losses, as the market can be highly volatile and unpredictable. Additionally, staying informed about market trends, technological advancements, and regulatory changes can help you make timely and informed decisions.

As you navigate the vast and often volatile world of cryptocurrency investments, understanding these critical criteria and trends will equip you with the knowledge to spot potential winners in the crypto space. This insight not only aids in making informed investment choices but also enriches your understanding of the cryptocurrency ecosystem as a whole, preparing you for future developments and opportunities in this exciting field.

In wrapping up this exploration of the factors and trends that could herald the next prominent cryptocurrency, we've traversed through a landscape where technology meets practicality; team expertise synergizes with community support, and market potential often dictates the trajectory. As we pivot to the next chapter, these insights form a bridge to understanding where the cryptocurrency market is today and where it is headed tomorrow. This ongoing narrative is not just about individual cryptocurrencies but about the broader evolution of finance and technology—a narrative in which you are both a participant and a beneficiary.

6.7 Knowledge Check: Test Your Understanding

What historical event significantly influenced the creation of cryptocurrencies, as discussed in the chapter?

a) The invention of the internet

b) The Global Financial Crisis of 2008

c) The launch of the first iPhone

d) The fall of the Berlin Wall

What is one of the key advantages of Decentralized Finance (DeFi) over traditional financial systems?

a) Higher transaction fees and slower processing times

b) The necessity for physical banking infrastructure

c) Elimination of intermediaries, leading to reduced costs and faster transactions

d) Complete reliance on government regulation

Answers:

1 – b) The Global Financial Crisis of 2008

2 – c) Elimination of intermediaries, leading to reduced costs and faster transactions

REAL-WORLD APPLICATIONS

As the dawn of cryptocurrency rewrites the annals of financial history, it isn't just the technology that astonishes but also the stories of individuals who have navigated this new terrain with remarkable success. These trailblazers have garnered substantial wealth through savvy investments and shaped the evolving dynamics of digital currency markets globally. Their journeys, diverse in approach yet unified by success, offer more than inspiration; they serve as a practical guide to the multifaceted world of cryptocurrency investing.

7.1 Real-World Success Stories of Cryptocurrency Investors

The cryptocurrency investment landscape is dotted with stories of ordinary individuals who have achieved extraordinary success. These investors come from varied backgrounds but share a common thread—a keen sense of the market and an ability to act strategically under volatile conditions. Consider the story of a young graphic designer from Chicago who turned a modest investment in Bitcoin into a fortune. Initially intrigued by the technology's potential to disrupt traditional banking, she purchased Bitcoin in its early stages at a low price. Her strategy was simple yet effective: buy and hold. She believed in the technology's future and held on despite Bitcoin's price fluctuations. Her patience paid off when Bitcoin peaked, multiplying her initial investment many times over. Her story is a testament to the power of long-term investment in a world where short-term fluctuations often deter the faint-hearted.

On the other end of the spectrum is a day trader based in Tokyo who mastered the art of timing the market with precision. With a background in finance, he leveraged his understanding of market indicators and trends to buy and sell cryptocurrencies over shorter periods. His approach was analytical and data-driven, involving meticulous research and real-time monitoring of market conditions. He generated substantial returns by capitalizing on small price movements and leveraging his quick decision-making skills. He demonstrated that a strategic mind can find immense opportunities even in the short-term whirlwind of crypto trading.

Another compelling story comes from a software developer in Silicon Valley who used mining to delve into the crypto world. Recognizing the potential of Ethereum early on, he set up a mining rig in his garage, using his technical skills to optimize the process. Mining provided him with a steady flow of Ethereum and a deep understanding of blockchain technology, which he later used to develop blockchain solutions for businesses. His dual approach of earning through mining and applying the acquired knowledge to build a blockchain consultancy illustrates how a technical skillset can be effectively utilized to carve out a niche in the crypto space.

These illustrative stories are narratives of financial gain and lessons in strategic planning, patience, and adaptability. They underscore the importance of understanding the market, recognizing one's strengths, and staying committed to one's investment philosophy. Moreover, these success stories have had a ripple effect, influencing countless others to explore the possibilities within the crypto market and contributing to the mainstream acceptance of cryptocurrencies as a legitimate investment class.

The impact of real successes extends beyond individual achievements. They have collectively contributed to the robust growth of the cryptocurrency market, attracting more investors and increasing the market's liquidity. As more people become aware of and inspired by these successes, the demand grows in size and sophistication, leading to more innovations and improvements in the ecosystem.

In essence, the real-world successes of cryptocurrency investors do more than fill the pages of a financial fairytale; they provide tangible proof of the opportunities within the complex matrices of blockchain technology. As more individuals venture into this realm, equipped with the lessons gleaned from these pioneers, the narrative of cryptocurrency continues to evolve, driven by a combination of technological innovation and human ambition.

7.2 Businesses That Thrive on Cryptocurrency and Blockchain

In the intricate dance of technology and commerce, cryptocurrency and blockchain have emerged as players and transformative forces, reshaping how businesses operate globally. Major companies across various sectors recognize the strategic advantages of integrating these technologies into their operations, moving beyond mere transactional uses to fundamentally enhancing their business models. For instance, global retail giants now use blockchain to streamline supply chain processes, improving transparency and efficiency. By maintaining a decentralized ledger of all transactions, these companies can track the provenance and status of each product, from manufacture to sale, reducing losses from counterfeit goods and improving supply chain accountability.

Similarly, several multinational banks have adopted blockchain technology in finance to facilitate faster, more secure cross-border transactions. Traditional methods, often cumbersome and slow due to intermediary processes and compliance checks, are being revolutionized. Blockchain offers a streamlined approach, where transactions are verified and recorded instantaneously on a secure, immutable ledger, drastically reducing processing times and transaction costs. This enhances customer satisfaction by speeding up transactions and positions these banks as forward-thinking, technologically adept entities in a competitive market.

Adopting cryptocurrency as a payment method is another strategic integration in significant businesses. A well-known electric vehicle manufacturer briefly allowed customers to purchase cars using Bitcoin, signaling a substantial endorsement of cryptocurrency as a viable payment method. Although the initiative was paused due to environmental concerns regarding Bitcoin mining, it marked a pivotal moment in accepting cryptocurrencies in mainstream commerce. Such moves by large corporations not only boost the legitimacy of cryptocurrencies but also encourage other businesses to explore similar avenues, potentially leading to broader adoption and innovation in cryptocurrency payment systems.

Startups, often agile and innovative, are inherently aligned with the disruptive nature of blockchain and cryptocurrencies. Numerous startups have built their entire business models around these technologies, venturing into sectors as diverse as healthcare, real estate, and media. In healthcare, blockchain-based startups are developing systems to securely store and share patient data among providers, enhancing the continuity and quality of care while ensuring patient privacy and data security. Real estate startups are leveraging blockchain to simplify and secure buying and selling property by digitizing deeds and other legal documents, making transactions more transparent and reducing the potential for fraud.

The economic impact of businesses adopting cryptocurrency and blockchain technology is profound. These technologies create new markets and revitalize traditional ones through increased efficiency and reduced costs. Job creation is a significant aspect of this economic impact. As industries adopt these technologies, there is a growing demand for professionals skilled in blockchain development, cryptocurrency trading, legal and regulatory compliance, and cybersecurity. This demand fosters a new wave of employment opportunities and contributes to economic growth, particularly in the technology and finance sectors.

However, integrating cryptocurrency and blockchain into business operations is not devoid of challenges. Regulatory uncertainty remains one of the most significant hurdles. The legal landscape for cryptocurrency is still evolving, with varying regulations across different jurisdictions. This poses a challenge for businesses operating globally, as they must navigate a patchwork of rules that can impact everything from how transactions are recorded and taxed to how coins are mined and stored. Businesses must stay agile, keeping abreast of regulatory changes and adapting their operations accordingly to ensure compliance and mitigate risks associated with legal non-compliance.

Technological challenges also abound, particularly in terms of scalability and security. Blockchain networks, like those of Bitcoin and Ethereum, are often slow when handling large volumes of transactions due to the inherent limitations of their design. While solutions like network upgrades and new blockchain protocols are in development, businesses must consider these factors when integrating blockchain into their operations. Security concerns, particularly the risk of hacking and data breaches, also require rigorous attention. While blockchain is highly secure, other aspects of cryptocurrency systems, such as wallets and exchanges, are more vulnerable to attacks.

Businesses that successfully navigate these challenges often emerge more muscular, agile, and better equipped to face the future. They reap the benefits of enhanced efficiency and new opportunities and contribute to these technologies' broader adoption and normalization in the global marketplace. As more businesses explore and integrate cryptocurrency and blockchain into their operations, they transform their practices and influence the global economic landscape, driving innovation and growth in the digital age.

7.3 Cryptocurrencies in Emerging Markets: Opportunities and Challenges

In the vibrant tapestry of global finance, emerging markets exhibit a unique pattern of cryptocurrency adoption, characterized by dynamic, rapidly evolving landscapes that challenge and reward stakeholders. These regions, often marked by economic volatility and infrastructural constraints, present a fertile ground for digital currencies, offering a paradigm shift in how financial transactions are conducted in countries where traditional banking infrastructures are either underdeveloped or mistrusted, cryptocurrencies are not merely digital assets but lifelines that offer both accessibility and new economic opportunities.

The deployment of cryptocurrencies in these markets often responds directly to local needs. For instance, in some African countries, where banking services are sparse and the unbanked population is high, cryptocurrencies offer a viable solution for financial inclusion. Mobile penetration in these regions is high, and mobile-based crypto wallets have become increasingly popular, enabling people to transact securely and efficiently without needing a bank account. This accessibility is crucial in regions where travel to a physical bank may be impractical or unsafe. Furthermore, in economies plagued by hyperinflation, cryptocurrencies provide a more stable store of value than local currencies, attracting users motivated by necessity and opportunity.

However, the burgeoning growth of cryptocurrencies in emerging markets is challenging. Regulatory uncertainty looms, with many governments in these regions still grappling with how to approach this new technology legally. Without clear regulations, both businesses and individuals face significant risks. On one hand, the lack of regulation can lead to increased investment, as stringent rules do not hinder companies and consumers. On the other hand, it can also lead to increased fraud and scams, as was the case in Uganda, where a lack of clear cryptocurrency regulations led to the proliferation of fraudulent schemes, eroding public trust.

Market volatility also presents a significant hurdle. While all cryptocurrencies are inherently volatile, this volatility is exacerbated in emerging markets, where unstable economic conditions and currencies are weak. This can deter new users from adopting cryptocurrencies, as the potential for dramatic fluctuations in value makes them a risky investment. Moreover, infrastructure issues such as limited internet access or frequent power outages can hinder the effectiveness and reliability of cryptocurrency-based solutions, impacting user experience and adoption rates.

Despite these challenges, compelling success stories highlight cryptocurrencies' transformative impact in emerging markets. Consider Venezuela, where rampant hyperinflation has rendered the local currency worthless, devastating savings and making everyday transactions complex. In response, many Venezuelans have turned to Bitcoin as an alternative currency. It provides a more stable store of value compared to the Venezuelan bolívar and facilitates transactions and remittances that are otherwise hampered by the financial system. Cryptocurrencies have offered a semblance of economic stability for many, illustrating a profound case of digital currencies stepping in where traditional financial systems have faltered.

Another noteworthy example is in the Philippines, where cryptocurrency adoption has been driven by the urgent need to enhance the efficiency of remittance flows crucial to the country's economy. Many of the population working abroad face challenges with slow and costly money transfers. Cryptocurrencies have emerged as a viable solution, providing a faster, more affordable remittance alternative. Collaborations between blockchain-based companies and local financial institutions have facilitated these transactions, ensuring compliance with local regulations while significantly reducing costs and processing times. This integration benefits individual users and strengthens the overall economy by ensuring that a more significant portion of the money sent home by overseas workers reaches its intended recipients.

These examples underscore the nuanced spectrum of opportunities and challenges cryptocurrencies present in emerging markets. They are not merely technological innovations but are tools for economic and social empowerment woven into the very fabric of daily life. As these markets continue to evolve, the role of cryptocurrencies will likely expand, driven by a combination of user needs, technological advancements, and the gradual maturation of regulatory frameworks.

7.4 The Role of Cryptocurrency in Enhancing Financial Inclusion

Cryptocurrencies, through their inherent decentralized nature, provide a compelling narrative for financial inclusion, especially for the unbanked or underbanked populations globally. These groups, often sidelined by traditional banking systems due to geographical barriers, socioeconomic status, or lack of documentation, find a beacon of hope in cryptocurrencies. The technology underlying these digital assets, blockchain, facilitates access to essential financial services by enabling secure and transparent transactions that do not require the intermediation of traditional financial institutions. This shift is consequential in rural or impoverished areas with sparse or non-existent banking infrastructure. Here, cryptocurrencies can democratize access to capital by providing a platform for saving, investing, and transacting, all facilitated through a simple internet connection and a digital wallet. This banking method bypasses the need for physical bank branches, reducing the barriers to entry for millions of geographically isolated or economically marginalized.

Moreover, the impact of blockchain technology in reducing transaction costs cannot be overstated. Traditional financial systems often impose hefty fees for essential services like setting up an account, transfers, and withdrawals, not to mention the higher costs associated with international transactions. These fees can be prohibitively expensive for low-income individuals, effectively locking them out of the financial system. Blockchain technology mitigates these costs by eliminating the need for intermediaries, such as banks and other financial institutions, which typically drive up costs. The direct peer-to-peer nature of blockchain transactions significantly lowers transaction fees, making financial activities more affordable and accessible. This cost-efficiency extends to microtransactions, which are impractical under traditional banking systems due to their high cost relative to the transaction value but are feasible and economically viable on a blockchain network.

Cryptocurrencies also empower marginalized communities by providing them with tools for economic participation and autonomy. For instance, consider a community in a developing country suffering from financial exclusion due to systemic issues or instability within the local banking system. Cryptocurrencies offer a stable alternative to volatile local currencies and an opportunity to engage in economic activities on a global scale. Women, who are disproportionately affected by financial exclusion, find particular empowerment in cryptocurrency platforms. These platforms offer privacy and security, enabling women to accumulate capital, participate in the economy, and achieve greater financial independence without societal or familial pressures that might otherwise curtail their access to traditional banking resources.

However, while the benefits are numerous, the risks and limitations of using cryptocurrencies for financial inclusion are significant and warrant careful consideration. One of the primary challenges is the requirement for digital literacy and access to technology. For cryptocurrencies to be viable, users must have access to the internet and computing devices and a basic understanding of digital wallets and transactions. This can be a substantial barrier in regions lacking education and technological infrastructure. Additionally, the volatile nature of cryptocurrencies presents a risk, especially for individuals and communities that may not have the financial buffer to absorb potential losses. The value of cryptocurrencies can fluctuate wildly, and while this volatility can yield high returns, it can also result in equally significant losses.

Despite these challenges, the potential of cryptocurrencies to enhance financial inclusion remains significant. They offer an alternative pathway to economic empowerment for millions of people worldwide. As technology continues to evolve and access to digital education improves, the integration of cryptocurrencies in enhancing financial inclusion will likely become more robust, providing a critical tool for economic equity and inclusion. This evolution will require collaboration between tech developers, financial experts, and community advocates to ensure that the benefits of cryptocurrencies are accessible to all, particularly those who stand to gain the most from their promise.

7.5 Case Study: The Impact of Cryptocurrency on Remittances

Remittances, representing the money sent home by migrants, constitute a significant financial inflow for many countries, particularly in the developing world. Historically, sending remittances has been dominated by traditional banking systems and money transfer services like Western Union and MoneyGram. These channels, while reliable, often come with high fees and slow transaction times, driven by the complexities of international money transfers and the layers of intermediaries involved. For instance, typical costs can range from 5% to over 10% of the transaction amount, depending on the originating and receiving countries. This scenario poses a substantial burden on migrants who are often working abroad to support families back home, and the high costs reduce the overall amount that reaches the recipients.

Enter cryptocurrencies, which have begun to play a transformative role in the remittance industry by addressing many inefficiencies associated with traditional methods. The decentralized nature of blockchain technology, which underpins cryptocurrencies, allows for eliminating intermediaries in the remittance process, significantly reducing transaction costs. For example, while traditional wire transfers can take several days and incur notable fees, cryptocurrency transactions can be completed within minutes at a fraction of the cost, regardless of the sender's and recipient's geographical locations. This speed and cost-efficiency make cryptocurrencies an attractive alternative for sending remittances.

Moreover, the transparency inherent in blockchain technology offers additional benefits. Each transaction is recorded on a public ledger, providing a clear, immutable history of transfers. This transparency builds trust among users and adds a layer of security, as it is nearly impossible to tamper with transaction records. This aspect is particularly crucial in remittance transactions, where the risk of fraud and errors can be high, especially in less regulated environments.

The real-world impact of cryptocurrency on remittances can be seen in several compelling examples. In the Philippines, where remittances account for more than 10% of GDP, many workers abroad have turned to Bitcoin and other cryptocurrencies to send money home using platforms like Coins. The Philippines allows users to convert cryptocurrencies into local currency, which can then be paid to recipients through traditional means or even withdrawn from ATMs. Using such platforms significantly reduces the cost of remittances, allowing Filipino workers abroad to send more money home, thereby substantially impacting their families' financial well-being.

In Africa, where remittance fees are among the highest globally, cryptocurrencies are also making inroads. Startups like BitPesa use blockchain technology to facilitate direct and cost-effective money transfers from abroad into African countries, bypassing traditional banks and money transfer services. This approach not only lowers costs but also reduces the transaction time from days to seconds or minutes, enhancing the convenience for users and providing immediate financial support to recipients.

However, despite these benefits, several barriers hinder the broader adoption of cryptocurrencies for remittances. Regulatory issues top the list, as many countries are still grappling with how to regulate cryptocurrencies. The lack of clear regulatory frameworks can create uncertainty for service providers and users, potentially limiting the adoption of cryptocurrencies for remittances. In some countries, the legal status of cryptocurrencies remains undefined, which can deter financial institutions from integrating cryptocurrency-based services into their offerings, fearing potential legal repercussions.

Another significant barrier is technology access. While mobile penetration is relatively high in many developing countries, access to reliable internet services, and in some cases electricity, remains challenging in rural and underserved areas. Since cryptocurrency transactions require internet access, their practicality is limited in regions with poor connectivity. Additionally, using cryptocurrencies requires a certain level of digital literacy, which can be a significant hurdle in less developed areas where education and technological training might be lacking.

Despite these challenges, the potential of cryptocurrencies to revolutionize the remittance industry remains vast. As technological infrastructure improves and regulatory frameworks become more apparent, migrants and their families will likely turn to cryptocurrencies for remittance. The continued growth and innovation in cryptocurrency and increasing global connectivity suggest a promising future for using digital currencies to enhance remittance efficiency, cost-effectiveness, and transparency. As this trend continues, it could have profound implications for global economic development, particularly in regions heavily reliant on remittances as a critical source of income.

7.6 Analyzing Failures: What We Can Learn from Cryptocurrency Flops

In the exhilarating world of cryptocurrency, the spotlight often shines on blockchain technology's staggering successes and transformative potential. However, the landscape is also scattered with notable failures—from bankruptcies and scams to flopped ICOs. Exploring these missteps provides an invaluable learning curve for investors and entrepreneurs alike, offering critical insights into what to avoid and how to foster resilience in this volatile market.

One of the most publicized failures in cryptocurrency was the collapse of Mt. Gox, once the world's largest Bitcoin exchange. This platform handled over 70% of all Bitcoin transactions at its peak. However, in 2014, it filed for bankruptcy following a massive hack where approximately 850,000 bitcoins were stolen. The root causes of Mt. Gox's failure extended beyond the hack itself. The exchange was plagued with operational mismanagement, a lack of proper security measures, and inadequate financial controls. The aftermath was a significant loss of investor trust in cryptocurrency exchanges, prompting a push for more stringent security protocols and regulatory oversight in the industry.

Similarly, the ICO craze of 2017 saw numerous projects raising millions of dollars through token sales, only to crumble and burn amidst allegations of fraud, poor execution, and regulatory pushback. As mentioned earlier, one example was the DAO attack, which targeted a leaderless venture capital fund operating on the Ethereum blockchain. It raised a staggering $150 million in Ether, but a vulnerability in its code allowed an attacker to siphon off approximately $50 million. This led to the demise of DAO and resulted in a contentious split in the Ethereum network. The failure underscored critical lessons about the importance of rigorous code auditing and the complexities of managing decentralized networks.

More recently, in November 2022, the cryptocurrency industry was rocked by the implosion of FTX, a leading cryptocurrency exchange. Unlike Mt. Gox, which was vulnerable to external hacks, FTX's downfall stemmed from internal mismanagement. Allegations surfaced that FTX misused customer funds and engaged in risky financial practices with Alameda Research, a crypto trading firm closely associated with FTX. These allegations triggered a wave of withdrawals that FTX couldn't handle due to a lack of liquidity. Consequently, the exchange filed for bankruptcy, leading its CEO, Sam Bankman-Fried, to step down.

The collapse of FTX sent shockwaves through the crypto market, resulting in a decline in cryptocurrency values and further eroding investor confidence. This episode underscored the critical need for robust transparency and strong risk management practices within cryptocurrency institutions. It also reignited discussions on regulatory frameworks aimed at ensuring consumer protection and financial stability in this rapidly evolving landscape.

These high-profile flops have etched a clear message: the need for robust security measures, thorough project vetting, and regulatory compliance cannot be overstated. For potential investors, these examples serve as a cautionary tale to conduct exhaustive due diligence on any cryptocurrency venture. Evaluating the viability of the business model, the track record and transparency of the team behind the project, and the legal landscape can mitigate risks significantly.

Moreover, the technology underpinning these projects must be scrutinized. Blockchain's allure often lies in its security and immutability. However, technological flaws can be catastrophic, as seen in the DAO incident. Continuous testing, community review, and staying updated with the latest in blockchain security practices are essential steps in safeguarding any crypto venture.

These failures give a broader understanding of the resilience required to navigate crypto. It's a sector where rapid innovation and regulatory landscapes continually evolve. Being adaptable, informed, and cautious can help stakeholders pivot and thrive amidst challenges. These lessons are about avoiding failure and building a robust foundation to withstand cryptocurrency markets' inevitable ups and downs.

Reflecting on these lessons helps paint a realistic picture of the cryptocurrency environment. It's a dynamic arena where the potential for high returns comes with significant risks. Understanding the successes and failures in this space is crucial for anyone looking to engage with cryptocurrencies, whether as an investor, entrepreneur, or enthusiast. By learning from past mistakes, the crypto community can strive toward creating more secure, sustainable, and prosperous ventures.

As we close this exploration of cryptocurrency flops, it's clear that these are not mere setbacks but pivotal learning opportunities that shape the contours of this digital frontier. They remind us that vigilance and informed decision-making are our best allies in cryptocurrency. Moving forward into the next chapter, we shift our focus from the pitfalls to exploring the essential tools and resources that empower cryptocurrency enthusiasts and professionals.

7.7 Knowledge Check: Test Your Understanding

What common trait is shared by successful cryptocurrency investors, as discussed in the chapter?

a) An aversion to technology and risk

b) A keen sense of the market and strategic planning

c) A background in traditional banking

d) A focus solely on day trading

According to the chapter, how have global retail giants utilized blockchain technology?

a) By replacing traditional cash registers

b) By creating their cryptocurrency for customer rewards

c) To eliminate all physical stores

d) To streamline supply chain processes and improve transparency

Answers:

1 – b) A keen sense of the market and strategic planning

2 – d) To streamline supply chain processes and improve transparency

MASTERING CRYPTOCURRENCY TOOLS

In the rapidly evolving world of cryptocurrency, staying equipped with the right tools is not just a convenience—it's a necessity. As you navigate the complexities of digital currencies, accessing a suite of tools that simplifies researching, tracking, trading, and securing your investments can significantly enhance your ability to make informed decisions and react swiftly to market changes. This chapter is dedicated to unpacking the essential toolkit every crypto investor should have at their disposal, from dynamic mobile apps to robust desktop platforms, ensuring you're well-prepared to meet the demands of the cryptocurrency market.

8.1 Must-Have Tools for Every Crypto Investor

The cornerstone of any crypto investor's arsenal is a comprehensive toolkit that addresses various facets of investing—from portfolio management to market analysis and security. Given cryptocurrency markets' inherent volatility and complexities, these tools are not just enhancements but critical components that safeguard and optimize your investments.

Comprehensive Toolkits

A well-rounded crypto investor's toolkit includes portfolio trackers, trading bots, and security tools. Portfolio trackers are indispensable as they allow you to monitor the performance of your investments in real time, track profit and loss, and analyze asset distribution across various currencies and platforms. Apps like Blockfolio and Delta offer intuitive interfaces where you can see a consolidated view of your crypto holdings, making it easier to assess your portfolio's health and adjust as needed.

Trading bots, on the other hand, automate the trading process based on predefined criteria and algorithms. In a 24/7 market, these bots help capitalize on opportunities even when you are not actively monitoring the markets. Platforms like 3Commas and Cryptohopper enable investors to implement sophisticated trading strategies, providing tools to minimize risk and potentially increase profitability through efficient trade execution.

Security tools are also paramount, considering the cyber threats in cryptocurrency. Investors should utilize reputable security solutions to protect their digital assets. Using encrypted wallets, secure private keys, and regular security audits can fortify your investment against potential breaches. Furthermore, integrating services like CipherTrace or Chainalysis can help monitor transactions and identify suspicious activities, thus enhancing the overall security of your cryptocurrency dealings.

Mobile Apps for Crypto Trading and Monitoring

The convenience of mobile apps in cryptocurrency trading cannot be overstated. With the market's fast-paced nature, having access to real-time data and the ability to execute trades on the go is crucial. Apps like Binance and Coinbase provide trading platforms and include features like price alerts, market news, and educational resources. These apps ensure that you stay informed and responsive to market conditions, irrespective of location.

Security within these apps is also a top priority; features such as biometric logins (fingerprint and facial recognition) and two-factor authentication are now standard to protect users' accounts and transactions. The integration of these security measures provides peace of mind, knowing that your investments are accessible yet protected by the latest in cybersecurity technology.

Desktop and Web-Based Platforms

While mobile apps offer convenience, desktop and web-based platforms often provide more comprehensive tools and functionalities for detailed analysis and trading. Platforms like TradingView or CryptoCompare offer advanced charting tools that allow in-depth analysis of cryptocurrency markets. These platforms support multiple time frames, a variety of indicators, and drawing tools that are essential for technical analysis, which is a crucial aspect of informed cryptocurrency trading.

Moreover, the ability to customize and save trading layouts and integrate market news and social feeds directly into the platform ensures you have all the necessary information at your fingertips. This holistic approach stimulates decision-making and enhances your ability to react quickly to market changes.

Integration with Traditional Finance Tools

For investors who manage traditional and digital assets, integrating cryptocurrency tools with conventional financial software is beneficial for a holistic view of one's economic health. Tools like Mint or Quicken that traditionally track bank accounts, investments, and loans can now incorporate data from cryptocurrency investments. This integration allows for consolidated financial tracking and analysis, providing a comprehensive overview of your financial landscape.

Establishing this integration often involves linking your cryptocurrency wallets and exchanges to these financial management tools. This can be achieved through APIs that securely transmit your financial data to the management platform, allowing real-time updates and insights. This simplifies financial management and aids in more accurate tax preparation, portfolio balancing, and financial planning.

8.2 Influential Crypto Thought Leaders and How to Learn from Them

In cryptocurrency, where the landscape shifts with dizzying speed, the insights of seasoned thought leaders can serve as both a compass and a map. These individuals, distinguished by their deep understanding and substantial contributions to the field, offer perspectives that blend visionary thinking with practical strategy. Knowing who these thought leaders are and how you can learn from their experiences is crucial for you, the astute crypto investor or enthusiast. It isn't just about following trends; it's about deepening your understanding of the market dynamics and the technologies that drive them.

Take, for instance, figures such as Vitalik Buterin, the co-founder of Ethereum, known not just for his role in creating the Ethereum blockchain but also for his thoughtful essays on blockchain technology and its broader implications. Then there's Andreas Antonopoulos, a prolific speaker and author whose works serve as foundational texts for understanding cryptocurrency technologies. Their backgrounds in programming and digital technology, combined with an apparent ability to communicate complex ideas to the public, have made their insights particularly valuable. Engaging with their published works through books, articles, or video talks provides rich knowledge to enhance your strategic thinking and technical expertise.

Leveraging the expertise of these thought leaders effectively requires more than passive consumption of their content. Engaging with their blogs, following their social media feeds, and attending conferences where they speak are proactive ways to connect with the pulse of the industry. Social media platforms like Twitter and LinkedIn are not just channels for updates but forums for dialogue. By actively participating in these spaces, you not only stay abreast of current discussions but also join a broader community of like-minded individuals who are equally passionate about the potential of cryptocurrency. This community can be a significant support, inspiration, and collaboration source.

However, while the advice and predictions of thought leaders can be enlightening, they should not be followed mindlessly. The fast-evolving nature of cryptocurrency means that today's truths may not hold tomorrow. Therefore, it's vital to cultivate the skill of critical analysis. When a thought leader proposes a bold new theory or investment advice, cross-reference these ideas with current market data and trends. Look for corroborating evidence from other respected sources and consider the counterarguments. This balanced approach to processing information will protect you from the pitfalls of hype and ensure that your investment decisions are well-informed.

Moreover, networking at blockchain and cryptocurrency events can be immensely beneficial. These events provide direct access to thought leaders and their insights and offer opportunities to engage with them in discussions, ask questions, and present your ideas. Building relationships within this community can open up avenues for partnerships and collaborations beyond mere investment moves, potentially leading to opportunities for developing projects or starting new ventures in the blockchain space.

By integrating these strategies, you position yourself not just as a participant in the cryptocurrency market but as an informed player capable of making strategic decisions that leverage the best of thought leadership in the field.

8.3 Keeping Up with Crypto: Best Practices for Staying Informed

In the dynamic world of cryptocurrency, staying informed isn't just an advantage—it's essential. With the market's rapid pace, developments can happen overnight, and the impact of global events can be immediate and significant. Establishing a routine for staying updated with cryptocurrency news is therefore crucial. This involves setting up news alerts through various apps and platforms to ensure you receive real-time updates on market changes, technological advancements, and regulatory news. Subscribing to leading crypto news websites like CoinDesk, CoinTelegraph, and CryptoSlate can also provide a steady stream of expert articles and analysis, helping you stay ahead of market trends. These sites often feature daily newsletters, which can conveniently absorb the latest information at the start or end of your day. Ensuring these updates are part of your daily routine helps integrate your investment activities seamlessly into your daily life, keeping you constantly alert to opportunities and risks.

Furthermore, understanding how to access and utilize analytical reports and market analysis from reputed crypto analysis firms can significantly enhance your investment decisions. Firms like Messari, Glassnode, and Chainalysis offer in-depth reports and real-time data analytics that cover a broad spectrum of metrics, including transaction volumes, wallet activities, and blockchain analysis. These reports provide a granular view of the market, helping you to understand underlying trends that are not apparent through surface-level news. For instance, an increase in large wallet transactions can indicate potential **whale** movements that may affect the market significantly, information that can be crucial for your trading strategy. Learning how to interpret these reports—recognizing the metrics most relevant to your investment goals and how they correlate with market movements—can give you a competitive edge, turning raw data into actionable insights.

The importance of continuous education in the crypto space cannot be overstated. The field is not only complex but also continually evolving, with new technologies and applications emerging at a rapid pace. Engaging with educational resources is vital to deepen your understanding and refine your investment strategies. Platforms like Coursera and Udemy offer comprehensive online courses that cover various aspects of blockchain and cryptocurrency technologies. Leading experts often develop these courses and provide a mix of theoretical knowledge and practical applications. Webinars and workshops, frequently offered by crypto exchanges and fintech firms, provide additional learning opportunities, often focusing on hot topics or detailed explanations of new tools and platforms. These educational resources enhance foundational knowledge and update you on innovative practices and emerging technologies.

Lastly, the impact of global economic and political events on the cryptocurrency markets cannot be ignored. Regulatory announcements, geopolitical tensions, or significant economic shifts can profoundly impact the market. For instance, regulatory news from major economies like the USA or China can cause substantial price fluctuations as traders anticipate potential restrictions or openings. Similarly, global economic events like changes in interest rates or inflation can influence investor sentiment in the cryptocurrency market, as investors may shift their assets between cryptocurrencies and more traditional investments like stocks or bonds. It is crucial to stay informed about these global events and their potential impact on the crypto markets. This involves tracking crypto-specific news and broader financial and political news. While not crypto-specific, platforms like Bloomberg and Reuters provide comprehensive news coverage, including economic and political developments that could affect cryptocurrency markets. By maintaining awareness of these broader events and analyzing their implications, you can better anticipate market movements and adapt your investment strategies accordingly.

In sum, staying informed in the cryptocurrency world involves a multifaceted approach: setting up efficient routines for daily updates, diving deep into analytical reports for nuanced insights, continuously educating yourself through various platforms, and keeping an eye on the global stage to understand external influences on the market. Each practice is crucial in crafting a well-informed investment strategy, ensuring you are reactive and proactive in your cryptocurrency endeavors.

8.4 Cryptocurrency Forums and Communities: Navigating Online Resources

In cryptocurrency's vast and varied landscape, forums and online communities are vital hubs of information, debate, and shared knowledge. These platforms range from the broad-reaching discussions on Reddit, where subreddits like r/CryptoCurrency and r/Bitcoin foster extensive dialogues and exchanges, to the more focused and immediate interactions within Discord channels dedicated to real-time cryptocurrency trading and developments. Specialized forums such as Bitcointalk.org offer a space for deeper dives into specific topics, technical issues, and development updates that appeal to those interested in the technical underpinnings of blockchain and its applications.

Navigating these forums effectively requires more than passive browsing; it involves active participation and a strategic approach to consuming and contributing information. To engage productively, start by understanding the specific etiquette that governs each platform. This might include the norms around posting frequency, the importance of sourcing your information correctly, and the general tone and rules outlined by community moderators. Engaging positively can increase your reputation and open up more meaningful interactions with other community members. It's also crucial to verify the information you come across; with the speculative nature of cryptocurrency, misinformation can spread rapidly. Cross-referencing facts with multiple reliable sources, checking historical posts on the topic, and using verified news outlets for any claims or data are good practices to cultivate.

Moreover, contributing to discussions can be incredibly rewarding. By sharing your insights, asking informed questions, or providing helpful answers, you enrich the community and deepen your understanding of complex subjects. Engaging in technical discussions or analyzing market trends can help cement your knowledge and perhaps position you as a thought leader in the community over time.

Understanding, navigating, and extracting value from these forums and communities is crucial. They are treasure troves of real-time market sentiment and grassroots insights that can sometimes provide early signals for market shifts or new technological advancements. Learning to gauge the community's sentiment—for instance, whether the majority sentiment on a forum is bullish or bearish on a particular cryptocurrency—can provide valuable insights into potential market movements. This requires a nuanced approach to reading posts and comments, identifying whether they are based on emotion or analysis, and understanding the broader context in which they are made.

Avoiding Misinformation: Teaching Strategies to Identify and Avoid Hype

Cryptocurrency investment's dynamic and often speculative nature makes it a fertile ground for misinformation and hype. Online forums and communities, while valuable, can also be echo chambers where unverified claims and excessive optimism or doom can distort reality. Developing the ability to discern credible information from noise is essential for making informed decisions as an investor. This begins with a critical assessment of the source of the information. Are they reputable, have a history of accuracy, what are their credentials, and do they provide sources for their claims? Answering these questions can help you filter out less reliable sources.

Moreover, understanding the common signs of hype and misinformation can guard against making impulsive decisions based on skewed information. Posts that promise guaranteed returns, pressure readers to act quickly, or rely heavily on promotional language should raise red flags. Similarly, information that seems out of step with broader market trends or not being reported elsewhere should be approached with skepticism.

To further hone your ability to filter information, engage with diverse opinions and perspectives. Echo chambers can reinforce existing biases, so actively seeking out differing viewpoints can provide a more balanced understanding of the market. This might mean participating in multiple forums, following various influencers with differing perspectives, or subscribing to various news sources.

Benefiting from Community Wisdom

The collective knowledge and experience of cryptocurrency communities can be an invaluable resource. Many members of these communities have navigated the highs and lows of the market and have insights that are not readily available through traditional sources. By actively participating in these communities, you can tap into this collective wisdom, gain access to practical advice, learn about emerging tools and strategies, and stay ahead of trends just starting to take shape.

To effectively benefit from community wisdom, be proactive in your interactions. Ask specific questions, invite detailed responses, contribute your experiences and insights to help others, and participate in community-driven projects and discussions. Many communities also organize virtual meetups, workshops, and seminars that can provide more profound learning opportunities and foster stronger connections within the community.

By integrating these strategies into your approach to navigating cryptocurrency forums and communities, you can enhance your ability to make informed investment decisions, avoid common pitfalls, and actively contribute to the vibrancy and resilience of the cryptocurrency ecosystem.

8.5 Advanced Resources for Crypto Analytics and Research

In the intricate world of cryptocurrency investment, where market dynamics shift with dizzying speed and complexity, gathering, analyzing, and interpreting sophisticated data sets is a fundamental skill for any serious investor. Advanced analytical tools and software provide this capability, offering insights beyond basic price tracking to include comprehensive data on transaction volumes, wallet activities, and even social media sentiment analysis. Among these tools, blockchain explorers like Blockstream and Etherscan offer a window into real-time blockchain transactions, allowing you to track wallet addresses, see transaction histories, and even observe intelligent contract interactions. Statistical analysis software like SAS or Python's Pandas library can be utilized to perform complex data analysis and predictive modeling, giving you a deeper understanding of market trends and behavior patterns.

Interpreting the data from these tools effectively requires a nuanced understanding of what the data points signify and how they relate to broader market movements. For instance, a sudden spike in transaction volume on a blockchain explorer might indicate a growing interest in a particular cryptocurrency or result from a single significant transaction. Distinguishing between these scenarios requires correlating transaction data with other indicators, such as market news or changes in wallet balances. Similarly, if a substantial number of transactions are directed toward an unknown wallet, it might suggest the accumulation of assets by a potential whale, which could have significant market implications. By mastering these tools, you can develop a more strategic approach to your investments, identifying potential buying or selling opportunities before they become apparent to the market.

Case Studies of Analytics in Action

To illustrate the power of advanced analytics in cryptocurrency investing, consider the case of an investor who used blockchain explorers to identify a pattern in the accumulation of a particular altcoin. By noticing that several large transactions were being directed to a few unknown wallets, the investor speculated that a major stakeholder was accumulating a significant position. This insight led them to increase their stake in the altcoin, which was subsequently appreciated when the stakeholder's involvement was publicly revealed. Another case involved statistical analysis to predict price movements based on historical volatility patterns during specific global events. By applying a quantitative model, the investor could reasonably expect the price drop during a significant cryptocurrency exchange hack, thus minimizing their losses by selling off their holdings just before the drop.

These case studies underscore the transformative potential of leveraging advanced analytics in cryptocurrency investments. They highlight the tactical advantages of informed decision-making and illustrate the strategic depth that data analysis brings to investment strategies, enabling risk mitigation and opportunity maximization in a volatile market.

Continuous Learning and Update

The field of cryptocurrency is characterized by rapid technological advancements and continuous evolution, which affects the tools and methods for data analysis. As such, a commitment to continuous learning is crucial for anyone relying on these tools to inform their investment decisions. This involves regularly updating your knowledge base, not just about the cryptocurrencies you are investing in but also the analytical tools and techniques at your disposal. Engaging with online courses that focus on new analytical methods, participating in forums where data scientists and financial analysts discuss trends in crypto analytics, and attending workshops and seminars dedicated to the latest software and tools are all effective strategies for staying updated.

Moreover, as new features and functionalities are regularly added to analytical tools and new tools are developed, keeping your software updated is crucial. This ensures access to the most accurate and comprehensive data and protects you against security vulnerabilities that could compromise your data integrity. In essence, in the fast-paced world of cryptocurrency, where data is as valuable as currency, your ability to adapt and learn continuously is directly proportional to your success as an investor.

By embracing the advanced tools available today and committing to a lifelong learning approach, you equip yourself with the knowledge and skills necessary to navigate the complexities of cryptocurrency investing. This proactive approach to education and tool utilization enhances your analytical capabilities and solidifies your position as a savvy investor poised to capitalize on the dynamic crypto market's opportunities.

8.6 Evaluating Cryptocurrency Investments: A Comprehensive Approach

A comprehensive approach is essential for effectively evaluating cryptocurrency investments and distinguishing sustainable opportunities from passing trends. Fundamental analysis forms the cornerstone of this assessment, focusing on a cryptocurrency's intrinsic value. This involves thoroughly examining the project's underlying technology, including its blockchain architecture, scalability, transaction speed, and security features. These technological aspects provide critical insights into the cryptocurrency's long-term growth potential and ability to adapt to evolving market dynamics and technological challenges.

Moreover, the team driving a cryptocurrency project significantly influences its prospects. A team with a proven track record in blockchain technology, strong industry connections, and a transparent operational history inspires greater confidence. The involvement of respected advisors further enhances the project's credibility within the cryptocurrency community. Community support is equally pivotal; a robust and expanding community indicates public trust, boosts adoption and fosters a supportive ecosystem.

Assessing the cryptocurrency's market potential is paramount. This entails evaluating the problem the project addresses, the size of its target market, and the competitive landscape. Projects offering innovative solutions to significant, widespread challenges tend to garner higher adoption rates and demonstrate greater sustainability. Evaluating legal and regulatory risks is equally crucial, as they can impact the project's operational scope and growth prospects.

Technical analysis serves as a strategic tool for timing investments. Investors can make informed decisions regarding entry and exit points by analyzing market trends and price movements using chart patterns and technical indicators—such as trend lines, support and resistance levels, moving averages, and volume changes. For instance, a moving average crossover may signal a potential reversal in price trend, guiding opportune buying or selling decisions. Interpreting these signals alongside broader market trends is vital for executing timely trades aligned with investment objectives.

Risk assessment is fundamental to a prudent investment strategy. Cryptocurrency markets are inherently volatile, necessitating techniques like asset diversification, setting stop-loss orders, and staying informed about news impacting market sentiment. Liquidity evaluation is also critical; higher liquidity facilitates easier buying and selling without significantly affecting prices, which is crucial for managing risks in volatile market conditions.

Crafting a personalized investment checklist is the final step in developing a robust investment strategy. Tailored to individual risk tolerance, investment goals, and thorough market research, this checklist incorporates criteria derived from fundamental and technical analyses. Key considerations include the practical application of cryptocurrency technology, credibility of the project team, performance in technical scenarios, potential legal or regulatory risks, and a comprehensive risk management plan.

By systematically addressing these elements, investors can construct a robust framework for evaluating cryptocurrency investment opportunities. This structured approach empowers informed decision-making that is aligned with financial objectives, enhancing the likelihood of successful investment outcomes.

In conclusion, this chapter has provided a comprehensive toolkit and strategic framework essential for effectively navigating cryptocurrency investments' complexities. You can monitor market trends, identify opportunities, and mitigate risks by mastering vital tools in portfolio management, security, and advanced analytics. Engaging with influential thought leaders and leveraging insights from cryptocurrency forums and communities enriches your understanding and strategic approach. Moreover, integrating a structured evaluation framework encompassing fundamental analysis, team assessment, market potential evaluation, technical analysis, risk assessment, and personalized checklists empowers informed decision-making aligned with your financial objectives. As you continue to explore the dynamic cryptocurrency landscape, adopting these practices will enhance your ability to thrive amidst volatility and capitalize on emerging opportunities.

8.7 Knowledge Check: Test Your Understanding

What is the primary benefit of using portfolio trackers for cryptocurrency investments?

a) To automate the buying and selling of cryptocurrencies

b) To secure digital assets against cyber threats

c) To monitor real-time performance and analyze asset distribution

d) To eliminate the need for regular software updates

What critical advice is given regarding the influence of thought leaders in cryptocurrency?

a) Follow their predictions unthinkingly to ensure success

b) Use insights to deepen market understanding while maintaining critical analysis

c) Rely solely on their social media posts for investment decisions

d) Avoid engaging with thought leaders to prevent bias

Answers:

1 – c) To monitor real-time performance and analyze asset distribution

2 – b) Use insights to deepen market understanding while maintaining critical analysis

Keeping the Knowledge Alive

Now that you have everything you need to start investing in cryptocurrency, it's time to share your new knowledge and help other readers find the same support.

By leaving your honest opinion of this book on Amazon, you'll show other beginners where they can find the information they're looking for and help them start their journey confidently.

Thank you for your help. The cryptocurrency world stays exciting and accessible when we share what we know – and you're helping me do just that.

Simply scan the QR code below to leave your review:

CONCLUSION

As we draw this exploration to a close, let's take a moment to reflect on the extensive journey we've traversed together in the realm of cryptocurrency investing. From the foundational layers of blockchain technology to the intricate strategies of advanced investment, this guide has aimed to transform you from a novice to a well-informed participant in the cryptocurrency markets. We've unpacked the complexities of digital currencies, delved into the mechanics of blockchain, and navigated through the multifaceted approaches to investing, all designed to empower you with the knowledge necessary to operate confidently in this space.

Throughout this book, we have emphasized the empowerment that comes from understanding. By demystifying cryptocurrencies and the technology that underpins them, we've equipped you with the tools and strategic insights necessary to make informed decisions. Whether choosing the right cryptocurrency, understanding market trends, or employing advanced trading tactics, the knowledge you've gained lays a solid foundation for confident participation in the market.

A recurring theme we've encountered is the imperative of continuous learning and adaptation. The cryptocurrency landscape is in constant flux, with new developments, technologies, and regulatory changes shaping the market daily. Staying abreast of these changes is crucial; it ensures your investment strategies remain robust and responsive.

I encourage you to utilize this knowledge to enhance your understanding and confidently navigate the cryptocurrency landscape. Engage actively with the cryptocurrency market, using the insights and techniques you've learned to foster financial growth and independence. Remember, the path to proficiency in investing is paved with informed decisions and strategic planning.

I also encourage you to immerse yourself in the vibrant community of cryptocurrency enthusiasts. Engaging in forums, attending meetups, and participating in discussions enhances your understanding and connects you with like-minded individuals who can offer support, insights, and partnership opportunities.

It's important to acknowledge the inherent challenges and volatility of the crypto market. While it presents significant opportunities for growth, it also requires a cautious approach. The strategies and precautions discussed are designed to help you navigate these waters safely, minimizing risks while maximizing potential returns.

Looking forward, the future of cryptocurrencies appears bright and brimming with potential. With each passing day, digital currencies continue to weave more profoundly into the fabric of global finance, heralding a new era of decentralization and financial democratization. As you venture forth, armed with the tools and knowledge from this book, you are well-prepared to participate in and benefit from this economic revolution.

Thank you for joining me on this enlightening journey. Here's to your success in the dynamic and ever-evolving world of cryptocurrency investing. Embrace the opportunities, stay informed, and approach each investment decision with confidence and careful consideration. The future is yours to shape.

References

Bankrate. (n.d.). *How to start investing in cryptocurrency: A guide for beginners.* Retrieved from https://www.bankrate.com/investing/how-to-invest-in-cryptocurrency-beginners-guide/

Investopedia. (n.d.). *Blockchain facts: What is it, how it works, and how it can be used?* Retrieved from https://www.investopedia.com/terms/b/blockchain.asp

Khatri, Y. (2016, March 14). *Bitcoin vs. Ethereum: What's the difference?* Investopedia. Retrieved from https://www.investopedia.com/articles/investing/031416/bitcoin-vs-ethereum-driven-different-purposes.asp

Wired. (n.d.). *How to choose and set up a crypto wallet.* Retrieved from https://www.wired.com/story/how-to-choose-set-up-crypto-wallet/

Vestinda. (n.d.). *Crypto investment strategy: Long term vs. short term.* Retrieved from https://www.vestinda.com/blog/crypto-investment-strategy-long-term-vs-short-term

HoneyBricks. (n.d.). *Ultimate guide to diversifying your crypto portfolio.* Retrieved from https://www.honeybricks.com/learn/crypto-portfolio-diversification

One Trading. (n.d.). *Crypto technical analysis: Techniques, indicators, and applications.* Retrieved from https://onetrading.com/blogs/crypto-technical-analysis-techniques-indicators-and-applications

Crypto.com. (n.d.). *Stop-loss and take-profit levels in crypto trading.* Retrieved from https://crypto.com/university/stop-loss-and-take-profit-levels-crypto

Coinbase. (n.d.). *What is cryptocurrency algo trading and how does it work?.* Retrieved from https://www.coinbase.com/learn/advanced-trading/what-is-cryptocurrency-algo-trading-and-how-does-it-work

Alpha Development. (n.d.). *Decentralised finance (DeFi) risks: How to safely protect your investments and navigate the crypto landscape.* Retrieved from https://alphadevelopment.com/insights/decentralised-finance-defi-risks-how-to-protect-your-investments-and-navigate-the-crypto-landscape-safely/#:~:text=Liquidity%20Risk%3A%20DeFi%20relies%20on,place%20for%20dealing%20with%20it

CoinDCX. (n.d.). *A complete guide to crypto futures trading: From basics.* Retrieved from https://coindcx.com/blog/cryptocurrency/crypto-futures-trading-explained/

Coin Bureau. (n.d.). *ICO vs. STO vs. IEO: Comprehensive guide to token offerings.* Retrieved from https://www.coinbureau.com/education/ico-sto-ieo/

Radyc, S. (n.d.). *Cryptocurrency security: Best practices for safeguarding your assets.* LinkedIn. Retrieved from https://www.linkedin.com/pulse/cryptocurrency-security-best-practices-safeguarding-your-radyc

Investopedia. (n.d.). *Hot wallet vs. cold wallet: What's the difference?.* Retrieved from https://www.investopedia.com/hot-wallet-vs-cold-wallet-7098461

Federal Trade Commission. (n.d.). *What to know about cryptocurrency and scams.* Retrieved from https://consumer.ftc.gov/articles/what-know-about-cryptocurrency-and-scams

Coinbase. (n.d.). *What is two-factor authentication (2FA) in crypto?.* Retrieved from https://www.coinbase.com/learn/wallet/what-is-two-factor-authentication-2fa-in-crypto#:~:text=This%20process%20seeks%20to%20prevent,security%20token%2C%20or%20mobile%20device

PwC. (2023). *PwC global crypto regulation report 2023.* Retrieved from https://www.pwc.com/gx/en/new-ventures/cryptocurrency-assets/pwc-global-crypto-regulation-report-2023.pdf

Sumsub. (n.d.). *Crypto AML guide: All you need to know in 2024*. Retrieved from https://sumsub.com/blog/crypto-aml-guide/

University of Florida News. (2024, February). *Regulation makes crypto markets more efficient*. Retrieved from https://news.ufl.edu/2024/02/cryptocurrency-regulation/

Fidelity. (n.d.). *Crypto tax guide*. Retrieved from https://www.fidelity.com/learning -center/personal-finance/retirement/crypto-tax-guide

VanEck. (2023). *11 crypto predictions for 2023*. Retrieved from https://www.vaneck. com/us/en/blogs/digital-assets/matthew-sigel-11-crypto-predictions-for-2023/

LinkedIn. (n.d.). *Decentralized finance (DeFi) and its impact on the global financial system*. Retrieved from https://www.linkedin.com/pulse/revolutionizing-finance-decen tralized-defi-its-impact-global-8d5zc

Forbes. (2023, November 13). *The future of NFTs: Will the market revive in 2024?*. Retrieved from https://www.forbes.com/sites/digital-assets/2023/11/13/the-future-of -nfts-will-the-market-revive-in-2024/

DAC.digital. (n.d.). *Blockchain for banking: Finance case studies*. Retrieved from htt ps://dac.digital/blockchain-for-banking/

Binance. (n.d.). *12 bitcoin success stories*. Retrieved from https://www.binance.com/e n/square/post/1188761

Forkast News. (n.d.). *81 of top 100 companies use blockchain technology*. Retrieved from https://forkast.news/81-of-top-100-companies-use-blockchain-technology-blockdata/

Forbes. (2023, December 24). *Bitcoin's rise as financial game changer in emerging markets*. Retrieved from https://www.forbes.com/sites/digital-assets/2023/12/24/bitc oins-rise-as-financial-game-changer-in-emerging-markets/

Brookings Institution. (n.d.). *Debunking the narratives about cryptocurrency and financial inclusion*. Retrieved from https://www.brookings.edu/articles/debunking-the-narratives-about-cryptocurrency-and-financial-inclusion/

NinjaPromo. (n.d.). *36 best crypto tools for analysis, trading & research in 2024*. Retrieved from https://ninjapromo.io/best-crypto-tools-for-analysis-trading-research

CryptoJobsList. (n.d.). *10 top crypto influencers to follow: Meet the elites in 2024*. Retrieved from https://cryptojobslist.com/blog/top-crypto-influencers

WalletInvestor. (n.d.). *How to identify and avoid fake news in the crypto industry*. Retrieved from https://walletinvestor.com/magazine/how-to-identify-and-avoid-fake-news-in-the-crypto-industry

U.S. News & World Report. (n.d.). *7 best cryptocurrency investing strategies*. Retrieved from https://money.usnews.com/investing/articles/best-cryptocurrency-investing-strategies